DEDICATION

To my mother and my father . . .
for being great role models while I was growing up.

To my three wonderful daughters . . .
who have taught me about finding true happiness
in motherhood.

I0878371

ACKNOWLEDGMENTS

My heartfelt thanks to:

My husband, for being such a supportive partner during the writing of this book and taking an active role in the lives of our daughters.

"Grandpa" Lowell and "Grandma" Helen Dawes, for watching the girls often, so I could spend quiet time writing.

My brother Randy, for saying "just write the book" and being by my side all my life.

Pola Firestone of BookWorks, for consulting on this book, helping me with the self-publishing process and pulling together a great team!

Kirsten McBride, for editing and giving good advice to keep me focused.

Steve Dittbenner, illustrator, and Lynn Dittbenner, designer and production coordinator, for making the vision of my book a reality.

Diane Brittingham, for typing a messy manuscript.

Sylvie Radvinsky, for retyping the edited version.

My pastors, Tom Sparks and Bob Field, for answering all my questions!

Dr. R.B. Beckmann, Dr. Anne Bray, Terri Clamons, Isabel Johnson and Dr. Jerry Matile, for reviewing certain chapters and the introduction. I truly appreciated all your advice and encouragement.

When MOM's HAPPY EVERY ONE'S HAPPY

A Guide for Improving Self-Identity and Relationships

Susan Dawes

OVERLAND PARK
KANSAS

When Mom's Happy, Everyone's Happy!
A Guide for Improving Self-Identity and Relationships
©1998 Susan Z. Dawes. All Rights Reserved.   2nd Printing July 1998

Cardinal House Publishing
P.O. Box 25096
Overland Park, Kansas 66225-5096.

Publisher's Cataloging-in-Publication
(Provided by Quality Books, Inc)

Dawes, Susan.
    When Mom's happy, everyone's happy : a guide for improving self-identity and relationships / by Susan Dawes. -- 1st ed.
    p. cm.
    Preassigned LCCN: 97-92503.
    ISBN: 0-9660242-0-6.
    Includes bibliographical references.

    1. Mothers--Life skills guides. 2. Self-realization. 3. Mothers--Religious life.   I. Title.

HQ759.D39 1997   646.7'00852
                            QBI97-1687

Printed in the United States of America

Cover design by Steve Dittbenner, Commercial Art Services
Interior design/production by Lynn Dittbenner, BookTech

Printed by Gilliland Printing, Inc.

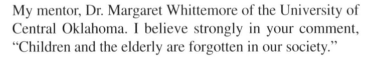

My mentor, Dr. Margaret Whittemore of the University of Central Oklahoma. I believe strongly in your comment, "Children and the elderly are forgotten in our society."

Three close friends, who listened to my own personal struggles through the writing of this book . . . Bruce Kerr, Sara Petersen, and Sandy Souyoul.

Susan Hargrave, for saying, "You write like you talk!"

Susan Ashby, who continually sent me articles to review and who wrote the closing poem.

All the kind librarians at Johnson County Library in Stanley, who so graciously and patiently helped me with the research.

KUDL radio station, for filling my house with music on happy as well as lonely days at a flick of the wrist!

Last, I am extremely grateful to all my friends and family who contributed to the writing of this book!

Susan Dawes

Table of Contents

Section One
Dealing with Yourself

Chapter I
Can I Do This? 7

- ◆ Dealing with the transition of staying home or returning to work
- ◆ Dealing with and recognizing loneliness, depression, and guilt

Chapter II
A Time for Growth and Self-Fulfillment 21

- ◆ Mother's happiness—A holistic approach: Mental, physical, emotional, social, and spiritual well-being
- ◆ Self-growth and fulfillment
- ◆ Self-esteem
- ◆ Goal-setting

Chapter III
Now Is a Time to Feel Good! 39

- ◆ Diet and exercise; behavior modification plan

Chapter IV
Balancing Your Relationships 57

◆ Working on your relationships with husband, friends, and children

Chapter V
You Deserve a Break Some Days! 73

◆ Treating yourself and enjoying your interests

◆ Finding support from others and groups

Section Two
Dealing with Your Children
Chapter VI
Will This Day Ever End? 101

◆ Normal days, rainy days, sick days, and winter time—What to do?

Chapter VII
Please Don't Whine, Scream, or Fight Today! 111

◆ Suggestions and creative ideas to deal with these issues

Chapter VIII
Pick Your Battles! 123

◆ Suggestions on how to deal with different stages and phases with children

Chapter IX
I'm Not the Maid or Short-Order Cook
Around Here!

Around Here! 149

◆ Teaching your children responsibility
and respect

Chapter X
Enjoy Your Children!

Enjoy Your Children! 163

◆ Suggestions for having fun with
your children

Conclusion 173

Bibiography 177

◆ Helpful sources for further reading

INTRODUCTION

This book has evolved out of my experiences staying at home for the last nine years raising three children. For eighteen months out of that nine-year period I was employed and enjoyed it very much. The book looks honestly at the emotions, feelings, needs and self-growth of being a mother today. It also explores how to deal with your children during these formative and challenging years. The book expresses my own experiences, thoughts and suggestions, as well as those of other mothers regarding this transition in their lives.

A lot of societal pressure is put on women today. And it comes from at least two directions. On one hand, you may feel you have put a lot of time, energy and money into your education and career and, therefore, be resistant to putting your career on hold. You may have the need to be out utilizing your skills in the workplace. On the other hand, many of us hear from our mothers' generation, friends, and some professionals that the best thing for the children is that we stay home.

Well, this is a book that supports all mothers no matter what they choose to do. As mentioned, I have tried both—I have worked and stayed home with my children. I feel that each woman has the right to choose whether to work or stay at home. And I believe that in some situations women must work for economic reasons, for their own personal reasons as well as to enhance their own self-esteem and self-identity. Therefore, I am not going to debate the issue of stay-at-home versus working mothers. Instead, I think we need to unite these mothers and dissolve the line of division that has come between them and that often makes mothers who work outside the home feel guilty.

This distinct line has caused a lot of unnecessary finger pointing. It is wasted energy and makes both sides question their decision of whether to stay home or go to work! Research reports that 42% of working and stay-at-home moms show signs of depression. I believe one reason that many working women feel guilty is that the majority of mothers who stay home or have in the past and the books written on the topic are quite adamant about the importance of staying home.

Commonly cited are opinions, and research findings from years ago when times were very different. Also, husbands and other mothers sometimes put pressure on women to stay at home with their children. As a result of such pressure, some women who stay home are frustrated, resentful and suffer from a loss of identity. Therefore, whether staying at home or working, some women experience guilt and repressed anger, which leads to depression.

Over the years, I have seen examples of mothers who stay at home all day that are models of parenthood while others are uninvolved, inattentive and emotionally divorced from their children. And I have seen mothers who work part-time or full-time and still manage to give their children boundless love and support and others who are stressed out and distracted.

Put simply, good parenting and good childcare (in or out of the home) is good for the children, while inconsistent parenting and inconsistent childcare is not.

Rather than leap to emotional and impulsive conclusions about the "right" or "wrong" roles for mothers, we should focus our energies on ways to help mothers (and fathers) ensure that their children's emotional and developmental needs are met, especially during the earliest years! As my child's pediatrician, Anne Bray, said to me one day, "We need more consistent care for our children."

My underlying belief is that women should start to help one another and not judge one another. We do not know each individual's personal feelings and thoughts or life circumstances. We should support each person's decision and then work with one another to help raise our children—identify those mothers in need of assistance and lend them a helping hand, including more mentoring programs to support single mothers and very young mothers. And provide more support groups for stay-at-home mothers.

In addition, we should focus our attention on improving and strengthening our childcare system. Strive to make it a national priority! Push for better federal, state, and local guidelines for consistent care for every child! Demand that we provide better training programs, and pay our childcare workers more money! Good daycare is too expensive for people on modest incomes; it should be subsidized by government or by industry, as it is in many European countries. Children are being grossly short-changed in our country today.

Advocate for all businesses—small or large—to be more understanding of employees with children. For example, businesses could allow job sharing, part-time work, tele-commuting, extended maternity leaves, etc. In fact, research supports the notion that if employers are more flexible and willing to work with their employees regarding childcare issues, they will have more productive, appreciative and happier employees. Let's move in this direction! Let's produce happy moms who produce happy children!

My theory is that whatever you are the happiest doing is the best solution for you and your family. Regardless of the path we choose, we all need support and information to help make it an enjoyable and rewarding journey for ourselves and our families!

Section One

Dealing with Yourself

Chapter I

Can I Do This?

Yes, you can! And the key to being successful during the transition to becoming a parent will be your happiness. This book as well as the support you receive from others and your own determination will put you on the right track.

I'm sure everyone can remember the month and what they were doing the first time they were told that they were expecting their first child or that their adoption application was completed. I'll never forget the words from Dr. Kallenberger on that sunny day in July, "Congratulations, Susan, you are pregnant! You are going to 'have a baby'!" Those three miraculous words! I remember hanging up the phone, standing there alone in my kitchen thinking—"Wow! Me . . . I'm going to be a mom." Then I had this explosion of inner happiness. My thoughts were, "I'm going to have a baby . . . a baby!!!" Of course, at that point everything was rushing through my mind and I had a smile so big you couldn't have wiped it off if you tried.

Immediately after this initial reaction, I started pondering about a few major decisions that would affect my future and the baby. Should I quit work? Leave a career that I really enjoyed and had invested a lot of time and effort in? Would John, my husband, be supportive of my decision to continue working or staying at home? What type of assistance would he provide for the baby? Who would watch the baby if I returned to work? Realizing there was some time to think about this in detail, it still concerned me, especially with all the publicity regarding inadequate care for children.

Then I began dreaming about what the child would be, a boy or a girl? What would that little thing look like? Oh, and a name. How would we ever settle on the perfect name for this child? And what about the nursery and all the other important preparations for a baby!

Well, the day finally arrived when our first beautiful baby girl was born. It was so exhilarating. I thought I was Super Woman, not wanting to take naps during the day because of the fear of missing something. I would take pictures, lots of pictures, write on the baby calendar, transfer the calendar information into the baby book, video, take more pictures, do lots of laundry, and on and on I went. The excitement lasted for about three months until I was so tired I could hardly see straight. I was beginning to tire of the baby's routine. I missed my job that I had decided to quit a month before the baby was born. And I really missed the daily communication with all the coworkers. I wished I had some family living around me. And I wondered if I would ever have a life of my own again.

At about this time, I remember peering out my window and envying my neighbor going off to work each morning. She was always dressed so nicely, walked so confidently to her car and would wave good-bye to her son and caretaker. I wondered what kind of decisions she would be making during the day and what exciting projects she would be assigned.

However, reality soon would literally stare me in the face, smiling with glee, and I would quickly rationalize to myself that I had made a good sacrifice. Therefore, my day would certainly be different from my neighbor's, although her decision was right for her. Even though I felt my decision was good for my child at the time, it still didn't dissolve those feelings that were beginning to surface.

The first feeling was that of loneliness. The cul-de-sac we lived on was big, but scarce of children during the week. The swing sets were all empty and no children were running from yard to yard like I remembered from growing up. I kept thinking this isn't the way my mother raised us four children.

Thirty years ago the majority of women stayed home. The neighborhoods were filled with children all day and the mothers would have coffee and visit over the fence. In 1960, only 18.6% of married women with preschool children were employed; this figure had risen to 30% by 1970, and to nearly 50% by 1982. However, today overall, 59.6% of women are in the labor force (U.S. Bureau of the Census, Nov., 1996). This is an enormous change in a very short time.

With so many women in the workforce and their children in some form of daycare, as a stay-at-home mother your social network is obviously very limited. Since I was a first-time mother and most of my friends were working, I wasn't sure where to begin to look for support. My sister-in-law, Peg, made an honest statement to me one day.

"I remember those years when the children were little," she said, "I just assumed I was to stay home and just be a wife and mother. I didn't think I should disrupt my husband's schedule to go out or do anything for me! They were lonely times until my friend convinced me to start doing things with the kids and for myself."

I reflect back and think she was so right. I fell quickly into the trap of just taking care of the baby's needs and the daily household chores and duties. As a result, I neglected both my own needs and my husband's, something I will discuss later on. Honestly though, I was beginning to lose my identity and my self-esteem was taking a slide downward. I had let many things go by the wayside that I used to enjoy. I wasn't even reading the newspaper daily. Some days I felt like my major decisions were whether I should feed Sara baby food peas or carrots. And when I would go to a dinner function, for example, I felt as though the only thing that came out of my mouth was issues regarding babies.

Soon my feelings of loneliness started to produce guilt. I felt guilty that I was not happy with my decision to stay home. I would look at my daughter and think, "You're such a beautiful gift that we have been blessed with and wanted for some time. I love you very much, but why am I not content with myself? What is wrong with me?"

When we isolate ourselves, have feelings of guilt and neglect our own needs, it's quite normal to become lonely and have feelings associated with depression. I don't think people like to admit or discuss depression; however, I think it is an issue that needs to be addressed.

A good friend told me honestly and in confidence while being interviewed for this book about her struggle with depression a few months after her son was born. She described feeling lonely, lethargic and sleeping a lot. She said she looks back now and feels that she was probably clinically depressed, but didn't know what was happening to her or where to turn for help. It was not just the "baby blues" or postpartum depression because it had persisted for several months with many symptoms of depression. Several women revealed that they also had symptoms of depression, myself included, and were afraid to admit it or dare mention it to anyone.

My friend overcame her depression by returning to work after the baby was nine months old. She said going to work pulled her out of her depression. So, working may not be all that bad!

I believe that whatever a mother is happiest doing is best for her and the children. Like my friend, I chose to go back to work two years after our first daughter was born. We had just moved to a new area and it became a very lonely and depressing time for me. I found the days to be so long and mundane. So at the suggestion of my mentor, Dr. Whittemore, whom I respected and whose opinion I valued, I returned to work. Working was the best therapy for me! However, I felt guilty because of the comments that some stay-at-home moms would make to me and that unapproving "look" I felt they displayed when I would tell them how happy I was to be back working and using my skills.

I continued working until six months after our second child was born. I resigned for two reasons: I wasn't really bringing home any income and I was not pleased with the care the babysitter was providing my children. The care appeared to be very inconsistent and I began to let the guilt feelings toward this issue overrule me. I realized that I could go through an array of sitters until I found the right one for the girls, or I could stay home and find ways to be happy and fulfilled doing this important job. I opted for the latter.

So, you see I have experienced both sides and I can relate to both the feelings of stay-at-home moms and of working mothers. I am familiar with the societal pressure that makes you question your decision about working or not working; the lack of affordable, quality childcare for your children so you do not worry about them; and the lack of support systems when your child is sick or you just need a break!

A journal article which appeared in *Pediatrics* (Sept. 1994) reported on a study of depression among mothers of small children, comparing those who were not employed outside the home with those who worked part-time and full-time. Symptoms of depression were found among 42% of the mothers. Two-thirds were dissatisfied with their current work role (in or out of the home) versus one third of satisfied mothers. Satisfied mothers were primarily those who worked part-time. In my interviews with women for this book, I found very similar results. Approximately one third adjusted very well and were content with their new role. The other two-thirds have struggled with their feelings toward this new role of motherhood.

Another study in *Developmental Psychology* reported finding a higher level of depression symptomatology in the mothers who preferred employment, but remained at home. Most of the scores reported a mild rather than moderate to severe condition.

The statistics above reflect our changing society and lack of a support system for both stay-at-home and working mothers. We have more women in the workforce than ever before. We are a much more transient society, with many of us living away from our families. The women I spoke with who adjusted well to the stay-at-home routine cited having many friends who were at home as well as mothers, sisters, aunts, cousins, etc., to help out. By comparison, the mothers who had a hard time adjusting to staying at home mentioned not having the support of friends, neighbors, or family. Many had husbands who traveled extensively, or were transferred often. Women who work have the same struggles and worry about who to call if they don't have family or friends to pitch in if a child is sick, out of school, or something unexpectedly comes up at work. And they have the constant guilt of wondering if they are doing the right thing by working because of what I call the "societal pressure."

I recall some of the comments I encountered when I was embarking on this new life transition. I heard quite often, "Get your rest now because you have no idea how your life will change!" No one ever expanded upon this comment or suggested a book to read to help me understand what was ahead. The other comment that was hurled at me quite often from a few friends and older women was, "You are going to stay home with that child, aren't you? You know I did and those are the most important years of their lives . . . and they grow up so quickly!" After hearing that comment for the twentieth time . . . I just wanted to scream and say, "Yes I know you think I should stay home, but were you really happy and content during this time?"

I really wish I would have asked this question of those who so kindly gave me their unsolicited opinion. Instead, I kept quiet and felt guilty for questioning my decision to stay at home. I assumed no one else must have felt the way I did at that time. However, I discovered in the writing of this book there are many women just like me. Women who question their decision to stay at home. And then there are those women who return to work and experience a lot of undue guilt by society regarding their decision to work and also have to worry about the lack of quality child care.

Since it appears that the majority of mothers have experienced some kind of depression, I thought it would be helpful to list the symptoms of depression so you would be able to recognize them.

Symptoms of Depression: persistent sad, anxious or empty mood; loss of interest in activities; sleeping too little or too much; fatigue; reduced or increased appetite; thoughts of suicide or death.

Postpartum Depression: Intense feelings of sadness, anxiety, or despair after childbirth that interfere with a new mother's ability to function and do not go away after a few weeks.

Postpartum Blues: Feelings of sadness, fear, anger or anxiety occurring about three days after childbirth and usually fading within one to two weeks (sometimes called "baby blues").

Many new mothers have periods of sadness, fear, anger and anxiety. It is important to remember that these feelings are quite common. They do not mean that you are a failure as a woman or as a mother, or that you are mentally ill. They do mean that you and your body are adjusting to the many changes that follow the birth of a child.

If the "baby blues" or symptoms of depression don't go away after a week or two, you may need to talk to your doctor, pastor, rabbi, or other religious advisor who can suggest resources for counseling and treatment. And don't be afraid to make that call or discuss your feelings with someone, because you are not alone. Even if your depression is severe, treatment is available to help you return to normal as soon as possible.

There are other feelings that mothers are faced with as well. I've heard many women say that they sometimes feel guilty that they are no longer contributing to the family income if they decided to stay home instead of continue their careers. That is an issue that probably haunts us all. It would be nice to have that extra cash some months. However, if you can afford to stay home and stay on budget, cut out some of the frills, and try to be at peace with yourself about that decision. Or think of a creative way to make some money. I have listed some suggestions for you in a following chapter.

So all of us who have young children probably agree that as we embark upon this new transition in our life, it will present feelings and issues that make us take a careful look at ourselves and our children. And the most difficult decision we all face is: "Shall I work or stay home?"

Dr. Jerry Matile, based on many years' experience of being an obstetrician-gynecologist, offered these rules for helping a mother with this decision.

1. Consider the finances.

It is unfortunate that a decision of this magnitude is often simply a money issue. To get a realistic picture of your financial situation, consider the following. First, take your after-tax income. Next, subtract what you pay for childcare (if you are planning to deduct this from your taxes this step is not necessary). Consider fringe benefits such as retirement plans and health insurance provided through your work. The amount you arrive at is approximately what you contribute to the family income.

By quitting your job, some expenses may decrease, such as transportation to work, clothing and noon meals. However, some expenses may actually increase when a woman does not work. For instance, if you become more involved with clubs, social organizations, golf or tennis lessons, etc., expenses can accumulate.

In exploring this issue, also consider the lifestyle that your family currently enjoys and the importance of material things to you and your family. For example, you may feel a responsibility to save for college for your children.

If the numbers don't add up to the kind of lifestyle you need . . . you may be a working mother whether you like it or not! Make the best of this situation!

2. Don't let others unduly influence your decision.

Everyone has an opinion and they always seem to offer it most freely when it comes to mothering your children! Your friends, mother and mother-in-law are not you and they are not in your situation. Only you can decide what is best for you. It may take courage to be the only stay-at-home mother or working mother among your circle of friends. Although your husband's opinion is valuable, even he cannot decide for you. Sorry—this choice is yours! If you need advice, get it from someone you respect and who does not have a vested interest such as a respected friend, clergyman or physician.

3. Consider your self-perception.

Do you feel that your best attributes are shown in a working environment or at home in a community environment? How do you perceive yourself? Many times our self-image changes over the years. Our priorities change as our experiences and situations change.

The once hard-driving, successful, career-oriented person may find that her goals are no longer related to the corporate dream.

4. No decision is permanent.

Often, we look at decisions with respect to job versus family as irrevocable. This is many times not the case, however, if a woman finds herself in a situation that is not fulfilling or rewarding, it is up to her to change that situation. If a step is missed on the corporate ladder, life experiences may more than offset this slight slip. Many women find happiness working part-time, and many others enjoy temporarily putting their careers on hold for child rearing.

5. Be happy with your decision.

If you choose to continue to work, or if you need to continue to work, do everything you can to be fulfilled in all aspects of your life. Just because you work, it doesn't mean that family joys aren't just as important! Enjoy each moment that you can with your children and family.

Likewise, if you have decided to stay at home with your family, don't be jealous of working friends with more money or seemingly more "exciting" lives. Be happy with your choice—and if you're not happy, then change the situation!

In the following pages we will explore ways that I and other mothers have found to adjust successfully during this period in our lives and find enjoyment and fulfillment for ourselves as well as our children!

So do you think you can do this? Sure you can! It will be a challenging but enjoyable time with many rewards and personal satisfaction!

Chapter II

A Time for Self-Growth and Fulfillment

> "Your happiness and fulfillment is a very important
> and crucial aspect in raising your children!"
>
> Quote by Ruby Seibert (my mother)

When Mom's Happy, Everyone's Happy! When I test marketed the title of this book to scores of people, I was amazed at everyone's comment. They would either break into a smile or chuckle and say, "Isn't that the truth!" And this was the reaction from both women and men of all backgrounds and ages!

I think my friend Annette summed it up the best while dining out with a group of our friends one evening.

She said, "I don't think women realize how powerful they really are in the family relationship." She expanded by saying, "We are the ones who set the tone for our family's happiness. Think about it . . . If we are truly happy and content with ourselves, then everyone usually is happy too!" None of us argued this point, we all agreed, whether we worked or stayed at home.

I also remember my neighbor, John, making an interesting comment to me one day. He said, "I just want my daughter to be happy! You know what I mean, Sue . . . Your kids are happy! I can see it in them." I walked away that day thinking he is right. My children are happy, my husband is happy and so am I!

However, it is something I work at and will always be challenged at. I don't want to paint a perfect picture of the Dawes household. We have had our share of trials and tribulations. But, we faced them, worked on them and grew immensely from them. And we have always adhered to the philosophy of taking each day and trying to be thankful and happy!

I know you are thinking . . . She cannot be happy all the time. You are right; we all have our bad days. And we all have PMS. Yes, PMS. I do not have to describe the week before the cycle. Ask any woman, and her detailed account of how her persona changes is pretty true for all of us. So, that week I go from being happy to being snappy! And I mark it on my calendar and let everyone know it's coming.

And some of us have work that stresses us out, and parents who may be ill or declining with age. We will have to struggle with many life circumstances at one time or another. But, amidst all of it, try to be happy and approach life positively, because life is too short here on earth not to enjoy it.

I am fortunate since I have had training in the helping profession and have studied and learned ways to first ensure my happiness and then to work on making my relationships with my husband, children and friends positive and fulfilling.

I was lucky, too, that my parents were good role models for happiness and self-fulfillment in their lives. My mother enjoyed being a mother; however, she developed her own interests and had an identity of her own. She was also very involved in her community, church and helped others. My father worked very hard, but always was there for his family. He found time to spend with each child and was always there to listen and give encouraging advice.

But even if your parents were not good role models in this respect while you were growing up, it's not too late for you to be that happy, positive role model for your children! Children learn by watching and listening. How many times do you hear them say, "I want to be like mommy" or "I want to be just like daddy," and then you see your daughter playing mom with her babies, or your son mowing the yard with his plastic mower while dad mows with the real thing!

It is true about parental modeling. We must model behavior that is responsible and healthy. And this is done by taking good care of ourselves physically, socially, emotionally, mentally, and spiritually.

The second greatest commandment says that we must love our neighbors as we love ourselves. We need to also love ourselves before we can extend this love to someone else. And then I believe we need to spread this love by helping others. This can be toward our husbands, children, neighbors, friends and those in real need of our help and love!

Taking a Holistic Approach

I truly think that if we love ourselves, then we can find fulfillment in our own lives! However, it may take some time and self-searching. My recommendation is that we explore the holistic model that is used in the helping profession.

This approach, which has been discussed for some time, is very simple, and makes sense. I remember learning about this model in my undergraduate work and thinking this is the way life should be lived!

It is a model I have adopted and have shared with many of my friends and family.

My hope is that you will value and remember it, too!

Holistic health enhances the well-being of the total person. The total person is the harmonious functioning of the physical, intellectual, emotional, social and spiritual dimensions of a person's life. The single most important function of the individual is to enhance and protect its well-being.

Each individual strives for a sense of coherence in which events are meaningful and manageable. Think of the holistic health model in terms of a circle. It integrates all dimensions of the total person—mental, physical, social, emotional and spiritual.

It emphasizes self-knowledge, taking responsibility for one's well-being and being honest and open in transactions with the environment.

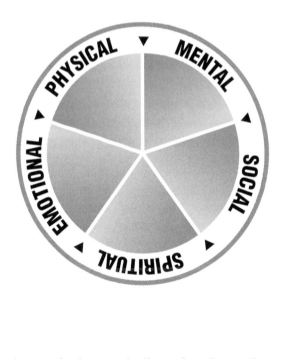

Let's now look at each dimension that makes up the circle to arrive at a potentially healthy well-being that exists in all of us!

Mental Well-Being

This pertains to the mind; tasks done or performed by the mind. It involves learning and memory. Learning and memory are closely related. Learning is represented by acquiring skills or knowledge, whereas memory reflects both retaining and being able to retrieve the skills or knowledge. That is, learning focuses on how the new content gets into the person; memory focuses more on filing and retrieving the content. You must always nourish your mind by learning new things. During my graduate studies I was fortunate to sit near a 70+ -year-old woman named Alice. I asked her why she was still taking classes! Her response was, "You are never too old to learn!"

She's right! Read, really read; research new projects, policies or causes; take classes; finish the degree you regretted not getting to; explore a new career or education path.

Be creative. Creativity is a part of the total mental process. In the simplest sense of a dictionary definition, *creativity* means having the ability or power to bring into being or produce things that are characterized by originality, expressiveness, and imagination. It is "the ability to develop new or different concepts, ideas, forms, structures, or products" (Chamberlain & Bergman, 1982, p. 112). I discuss many ways to nourish your mental well-being in Chapter V.

Physical Well-Being

The concept of health and wellness as encompassing mind-body unity reaches back thousands of years to

Middle-Eastern religions, the ancient Greeks, and Far-Eastern philosophies. According to this view, mind and body are not separated but seen as interrelated and interdependent.

Regular exercise is of importance in the prevention of illness and in the enhancement of health. It has both physiological and psychological benefits. Advantages that have been associated with regular exercise include: a greater ability to concentrate, a reduced risk of heart attack, more energy, reduced anxiety and depression, better sleep, better control of body weight, and an overall improvement in self-image.

So start exercising if you haven't already. Talk to your doctor first, if you have any health problems or questions. Begin a walking program, swim, ride a bike, play tennis, golf, or run. Pick a form of exercise that you enjoy! And do it at least three times a week! More information will be given on physical well-being in Chapter III.

Emotional Well-Being

Pain and pleasure enable us to strive and grow in ways that enhance the existence of self. Our emotions are an important source of information for alerting us to actual or anticipated danger and conversely assuring us of safety. Potential physical and psychological harm is signaled by the negative emotions of fear, anger, sadness and guilt. Events evoking these emotions can be seen as threats or challenges. Using events as opportunities to learn and grow leads to mastery and coping behavior. For instance, if we use opportunities like moving to a new area or grieving the loss of a parent as a means of growth, then hopefully we can face this with more strength the next time as well as help others through similar difficulties in life.

The positive emotions of interest and joy are sources of pleasure that motivate individuals to seek experiences that nurture and enhance their well-being. A healthy person is one who is able to make creative use of the positive and negative emotions. Pleasure and pain are integrated to strive for that which will satisfy the physical and psychological needs without seriously denying or harming others.

Social Well-Being

During the past decade, numerous studies have demonstrated the importance of social support for mental and physical health. Social support is considered to be more directly related to health and well-being. *Social support* can be defined as the subjective feeling of belonging, of being accepted, loved, esteemed, valued and needed for oneself, not for what one can do for others. Throughout the social support literature, the following types of support are proposed: emotional support, instrumental aid, informational support, and affirmation. The type of support that is beneficial at any given time may vary, depending on the nature and stage of the confronting situation.

Emotional support (encouragement, empathy) may help in depressing circumstances such as a loss of a child or parent, whereas *informational support* may be more useful in assisting an individual to understand how to relate effectively with his or her friends. *Instrumental aid* provides assistance with specific tasks, such as the preparation of nutritious meals or the transport of children to recreational activities. Finally, *affirmation* helps individuals to realize their own strength and potential.

Psychologically, social support may provide a sense of meaning to life or be associated with more positive affective states, such as improved sense of self-worth and increased sense of control. Social support is related to decreased stress during times of life crisis. A life crisis can consist of many things such as a loss of a child, an ill child, loss of a parent, job changes, divorce or separation, or maybe a long-term health condition that you are struggling with on a daily basis. Whatever the case, all mothers need some type of support during these trying times. Your husband should be a good source of emotional and social support. However, we need others— mothers, friends, neighbors, church members, and support groups—to be in place if we need them.

Spiritual Well-Being

I discuss this last, however, in actuality, it should have been the first aspect discussed and be seen as the center of the other areas. My pastor, Tom, pointed that out to me one day while discussing my book. Spiritual health is the ability to develop one's spiritual nature to its fullest potential, including the ability to discover and articulate one's basic purpose in life, to learn how to experience love, joy, peace, and fulfillment, and how to help ourselves and others achieve their fullest potential. Assessing spiritually goes beyond inquiring about a person's membership in a particular religion and taps deeper beliefs and feelings about the meaning of life, love, hope, forgiveness, and life after death!

Connectedness is an important part of spirituality and includes being connected with a larger purpose in life. Religious or philosophical beliefs such as commitment to humankind or trust in God put life in perspective and provide a reason for living.

If you have already found that true fulfillment for your spiritual well-being, good for you! And if not, begin by finding a church, synagogue or other place of worship, you feel comfortable going to with your family. Talk to your pastor, rabbi or religious advisor about books to read in developing your faith. Get involved in the life of the church! Learn from other role models in the church.

As we have seen in the preceding pages, holistic health is a state of well-being and vitality that brings an optimal level of mental, physical, emotional, social, and spiritual functioning. In this state, you experience a sense of joy, wonder, and love toward your self and the world.

So evaluate these areas in your life to determine if you are satisfied and fulfilled.

You should have no problem becoming that whole person. If not, this book will suggest in chapters to come how to find happiness in these areas of your life.

Growth and Self-Fulfillment

Now, let's move toward personal growth and self-fulfillment, which helps you accomplish an overall well-being. Psychologist Abraham Maslow's ideas on human potential are closely related to growth. By *growth*, Maslow means the development of capacities, talents, creativity, wisdom and character. This inner core, or self, grows into adulthood, only partly by discovery, uncovering and accepting of what is already there.

> *Partly it is also a creation of the person herself. Life is a continual series of choices for the individual... every person is, in part, 'her own project' and makes herself.*

Abraham Maslow

Growth, then, is a progressive process to increase that which already exists and to create that which is new for the purpose of enhancing the well-being of the individual. Growth refers to a personal change in a desired direction. This change may be sudden or gradual, but the movement is always in the direction of increasing possibilities. For example, an individual shows growth when she becomes more knowledgeable and capable, insightful and discerning, productive and creative, appreciative and responsive, accepting of self, and responsible to others. In short, it is the process of nurturing and creating personal characteristics toward becoming a more fully functioning person. Therefore, one's total well-being is sought through integrating the physical, mental, emotional, social and spiritual dimensions of living.

Self-knowledge and self-acceptance are the most important roads to self-actualization. Courage, integrity, and self-respect are important to continual growth! Stress and challenge are growth-producing, but only if they do not exceed personal limits. Remember, prioritize what is really important to you and don't over-commit. Discipline and a certain amount of control are essential. Learn to say "No" when necessary! Don't try to be "Super Mom." "Take time to smell the roses" as my husband's 90-year-old grandmother used to remind us every time we visited her home. That means treat yourself well, develop and enjoy your interests.

Risk is an essential feature of self-growth. "Nothing ventured, nothing gained" is a truism applicable to personal growth. Without taking chances, there is simply no way to grow. Risking is making choices, taking the next step, choosing which turn in the road to take, and moving on. The healthy, spontaneous person reaches out to the environment in wonder and interest, not without fear, and moves into the unknown and the future in spite of fear and resistance (Peck, 1978). When we extend ourselves, the self enters new or uncertain territory. The self becomes changed, enlarged, enriched or reshaped. We risk and we grow from the experience.

A pathway for personal growth must include an inner and outer journey. Yankelovich (1981) clarified the erroneous implication of self-fulfillment that the seat of sacredness lies wholly within the self. It also lies beyond the self if one is to reach that which is sacred and expressive. *Sacred* here is not used in its strictly religious meaning nor as the opposite of secular. It is used to mean that people and objects are valued for themselves apart from any purpose they serve. For example, running and gardening can be pursued purely for their practical benefits. But they can also become a sacred ritual, valued for their subjective feelings such as exhilaration of running or a deep attachment to that which is grown. When relationships and objects are valued only for their practical benefits, they are more likely to be impersonal, manipulated and downgraded. People and objects become sacred when they are valued for themselves, not solely on what they can do for you.

Yankelovich has noted a significant trend in persons looking for closer ties to others. "People feel good about themselves when they believe what they are doing is good for others as well as for themselves when they believe it is morally right." Therefore, self-fulfillment and growth can bring about a better balance between the duty to self and duty to others.

A pathway for personal growth is reached by developing a sense of worth and a sense of competence. Both of these are essential for positive self-esteem. Affirming one's worth requires a positive self-identity and constructive relationships with others. Personal feelings and values are important to an identity that sees life as meaningful.

I think mothers sometimes lose their identities and therefore suffer from lower self-esteem, particularly when they are not working. Let me give you an example.

A close friend disclosed to me one day that she felt as though she had lost her identity. She was married to a man who was very successful in his job. As a result of his career, she was expected to attend many social functions and entertain his clients. At first it was fun being "Mrs. Smith," decorating her house and going on shopping sprees. She also became the kids' room parent, PTA secretary, cub scout mother and car pool chauffeur to all their activities. She suddenly realized that she was Mr. Smith's wife and the Smith children's mother. The honest truth was she wasn't happy just being a wife and mother. You see, while doing all this, she wasn't exploring new avenues for herself or taking risks. She wasn't searching out new growth opportunities for self-fulfillment and felt very stagnant in her life, with no direction. However, after making some suggestions, she is now "Carol Smith," teacher, artist, wife and mother.

I think it is very easy to lose your identity when you stay home. I know, I've lost mine a couple of times. However, I think working mothers can lose their identities, too. They work hard at their jobs and then come home to care for the children and all the other household duties. You need to squeeze some time in for yourself, too!

Therefore, I recommend to you—set some goals for yourself starting today! Think about your hopes, aspirations and dreams! Write them down and devise a plan to reach them. Your plan should include long-term and short-term goals. For example, your yearly list may include these areas:

Personal

- Exercise at least four times per week (running, walking or working out at the gym).

- Take piano lessons.

- Attend a free lecture series.

- Take a class at the junior college for fun or to brush up on skills.

- Read the Bible more (begin with Psalms or Proverbs).

- Take a weekend away shopping with a girlfriend.

- Be a more patient and interactive mother.

Family

- Be more attentive and communicative with your husband (plan a weekly date).

- Spend more time individually with your children (take one to lunch or the library, etc.).

- Take two overnight mini-trips or a four-day vacation with your husband.

- Take a summer vacation—maybe camping at a lake or a weekend to a city visiting the zoo or museum.

School and Community

- Volunteer to help in the classroom when time is available.

- Volunteer to help on a certain committee for PTA and attend meetings.

- Call an older person once a week.

- Volunteer for an organization that can use your skills and talents.

- Teach Sunday School and Bible School.

- Serve on at least one church committee.

Long Term

- Finish your degree or take continuing education classes.

- Plan a trip to Washington, D.C., with your family in five years.

Use this as a guide to set your goals. Write them down and post them inside a cupboard door or somewhere else where you will be able to see them often and be reminded of what is to be completed. Strive to reach your goals! However, these are not written in granite, so don't feel bad if you don't accomplish every one.

Pathways to personal growth lead in many directions, but the ultimate destination is fulfillment of one's potential as a human being. This path may be blocked by danger and restriction of freedom. Inner strivings for growing in healthy, positive ways are guided by reason and emotion to protect the individual and to enhance its creation. More than one pathway exists to achieving our destiny. A spiritual dimension unfolds to direct the person toward a life of quality and purpose.

However, every person has to have certain conditions for making progress. Encouragement from others empowers us to cope with obstacles and master challenges. Values motivate and direct our functioning as an internal compass and a source of energy. Ultimately, the responsibility for our own destiny and choosing the path that enables us to be a more fully functioning person is ours!

Life is made up of being and doing. Being is living what one is, and doing is acting on what one wants to become. The inner strivings that take one along life's journey seek a sense of worth as a human being and competence to master or cope with whatever is encoutered along the way.

> *Whatever we believe about ourselves is what we become.*

J. Melvin Witmer (1985)

Happiness comes from within yourself. It does not come through material possessions, gaining more status or receiving it from another person. Real happiness is feeling fulfilled in all aspects of your life—mental, physical, emotional, social and spiritual—which promotes your overall well-being as a total person!

> *Happiness is something we create in our minds—*
>
> *It's not something you search for and so seldom find.*

Helen Steiner Rice

Chapter III

Now Is a Time to Feel Good!

This is a time when you need to feel good! In fact, you should always take care of yourself, watch your diet and exercise routinely. If you do exercise and have a healthy diet, you will have a better self-image, be more patient with your children and have more energy to put into relationships.

If you have never had experience with a weight problem, it is hard for you to imagine what a woman really feels like if she needs to lose some pounds. However, if you are struggling with some extra weight, you will be able to relate to this. I have experienced first-hand a weight problem during my senior year in college—gaining over twenty pounds in a few months. And no, it was not the freshman fifteen carried over! It was due to stress in different areas of my life. Instead of exercising to reduce my stress, I chose to eat. And eat, I did. I would eat three square meals, plus snack on candy—two chocolate bars at once, lots of soda, cookies, about anything to give me that instant self-gratifying moment. However, those self-gratifying moments would end and leave me feeling even more lousy. I usually felt sick in my stomach and would then realize that my diet had been blown again! It became a vicious cycle.

Quite frankly I didn't like myself very much during this time. I became lethargic—just did what I had to get by. I didn't go out much because I didn't like my appearance.

I became envious of other people because they looked better, were happier, and had more energy!

Then winter quarter rolled around. Thank goodness for winter quarter, Dr. Simmons, and the behavior modification course offered. Dr. Simmons challenged us all to pick an area we would like to change about ourselves. Some people chose to quit smoking, others selected to improve a relationship, and I chose weight control! This weight had to come off! And so far, three children later, I have successfully kept the weight off by practicing some valuable information and applying specific techniques.

Losing Weight Through Behavior Modification

Let us start with an introduction to the practice of behavior modification. This practice consists of applying basic learning principles to a diverse range of behaviors. We will look at *what*-questions: What is the person doing? Under what conditions are particular behaviors being performed? What are the effects of those behaviors? What reinforcers can be supplied? Most importantly, what does the individual want and what are the most efficient and effective means to help her?

Thus, the goals of behavior modification are specifically to decrease maladaptive, undesired behavior and increase adaptive, desired behavior. The purpose of behavior modification can be summarized in the following way:

1. To maximize the control an individual has over himself or herself and over the environment

2. To maximize the development and use of one's own abilities as well as environmental opportunities

While behavior can be changed without keeping any records, maintaining objective data on the target behavior before, during and after intervention usually makes successful change more likely.

Since the goal of behavior change is generally to increase or decrease behaviors, recording is directed toward giving clear evidence that the direction and duration of such changes are compatible with the interventive goals. Quite simply, recording is used because it has been found to be the most effective, accurate way of determining the efficiency and effectiveness of behaviorally oriented interventions.

So let's begin. But before we go any further, ask yourself if you like your extra weight. If you do, keep it, love it and drop the subject. But, if you don't, and you're ready to get real about weight loss, this may be your chapter.

Baselining

For the next week, write down on a daily basis everything you are eating, what time of day, what you are doing, why you are eating, when you are eating and how. Now let's take that information and analyze it.

Are you eating between meals, after dinner, before bedtime? What are you eating? Are you eating healthy or junk-type foods? Why are you eating? Are you really hungry? Or are you bored? Nervous? Depressed? Just being polite?

Some of us starve ourselves all day, only to raid the fridge in the wee hours. How you are eating is important. We often tend to "eat on the run" or just "grab a bite." When we do, we may wind up overeating. It takes twenty minutes for your stomach to tell your brain you're full. So slow down and enjoy each meal. Try to ask yourself the real reason why you are eating—and don't be afraid to say "No" when you're really not hungry.

Intervention

Now that we have the baseline information, let's implement the intervention plan, which will consist of recording, setting goals, devising a plan and rewarding yourself.

Take a look at a few important reminders before we begin:

- Use self talk. For example, tell yourself . . . "You can do this." "You will do this!"

- Drink at least six glasses of water daily.

- Do not eat anything after you have eaten the evening meal, unless it is a piece of fruit or plain vegetables or drink a glass of water.

- Eat three meals a day and two snacks a day.

- Have gum available to chew to curb the hunger pains when it is getting close to a meal.

- Continue to record everything you eat.

- Set a short-term goal every week. For example if I eat properly and exercise, I will treat myself at the end of the week (to a movie, browse in a bookstore, etc.).

- Have a long-term goal in mind. If I successfully lose weight in two, four, six months, I will buy myself some new clothes or something I really want for myself.

- Analyze your baseline information and determine when and why you are eating inappropriately. Then start your intervention plan.

SAMPLE CHART   Make one for each day.

Weight Intervention Plan

WEIGHT _____

DATE _____

BREAKFAST _____

_____

_____

SNACK _____

_____

LUNCH _____

_____

_____

SAMPLE CHART   Make one for each day.

MIDDAY SNACK   _____

                _____

DINNER   _____

                _____

                _____

GLASSES OF WATER _____

FORM OF EXERCISE _____

                _____

MINUTES   _____

                _____

                _____

A Stable Weight—Elusive, But Important

Now let's talk about a healthy diet plan. Most of us have experienced the distress of unwanted weight gain or loss. You may have struggled to lose extra pounds only to watch in dismay as your weight returns. Or perhaps you have the opposite problem: struggling to keep pounds on.

No matter which end of the weight spectrum you are at, this chapter addresses some important emotional and behavioral issues to help make weight maintenance easier.

A Range, Not a Number

With the help of your doctor or registered dietitian, begin by establishing a healthy weight range for you. Find a personal weight range that fits you and is reasonable given your family weight patterns, body type, age, lifestyle, and previous weight history. And remember, because of your genetic make-up, you may never be able to achieve the "model look." So do not set unrealistic goals for what you want to look like.

Your personal weight range may not fit your "ideal" body image, but it can allow you to succeed at weight maintenance. A range will also provide you with your own personal comfort zone. It's best to have a five-pound range within which your weight can vary. This is because small weight fluctuations are normal, especially for women at different phases of their menstrual cycle. You may be used to jumping on the scale each time you have eaten or exercised. It's better to weigh yourself once every week or two at the same time of day, preferably mornings, using the same scale, and wearing similar clothing. Only when you reach either end of your range do you need to modify your weight management tactics. A written weight record will help you keep tabs.

Balance, Variety, Moderation

Determining what to eat to maintain your weight can make you anxious. While balanced eating and moderation are necessary for safe weight maintenance, if you are a long-time dieter, the idea of eating certain things may bring up feelings of hunger and deprivation. These fears are natural because most diets do result in feelings of deprivation. Also, embarking on a new eating plan, even if it's not a restrictive diet, can be scary. However, a low-fat, high-complex-carbohydrate diet including plenty of fruit, vegetables, and grains will help you preserve your weight where you want it without undue hunger. This is because you can eat more of these foods than of higher-fat ones and still maintain your weight.

Making gradual dietary changes is easier and feels better than trying to change everything at once. Start with one or two simple substitutions, such as having fruit in place of pastry once during the day or using a lower-fat milk on your cereal.

Rather than eliminating rich foods from your diet, learn to balance higher-fat foods with those lower in fat. If you want a piece of apple pie for dessert, have a lower-fat main course such as steamed vegetables, beans, and rice. Learn what constitutes a serving size of various foods and create meals that are both healthful and appealing to you.Sometimes you may feel overwhelmed by a large quantity of food. If you buy a cake or a quart of potato salad, divide it into serving-size portions, wrap the portions separately, and store the food that you aren't going to eat immediately. If you eat at a restaurant and the servings are large, get a doggie bag at the beginning of the meal and put aside the extra food. If you find yourself facing an enormous buffet, eat small amounts of five or six items rather than trying to sample everything. Moderation is a key to successful weight maintenance.

Be sure to eat a wide variety of foods and spices that you like, so you will be less likely to get bored and stray from your food plan. Work with your registered dietitian to design an individualized eating plan that takes into account your particular needs.

Identify Emotional Eating and Find Non-Food Solutions

It can be very confusing to try to sort out when you are truly hungry and when you are eating for emotional reasons. Sometimes we confuse being tired or bored with being hungry. Perhaps you graze through the refrigerator when you are alone. Or you may eat when you are anxious or upset and feel better after eating. In these cases, you aren't really hungry, but eating has a calming effect. Most emotional eating can throw off efforts to maintain a stable weight by taking in extra "unneeded" food.

Identifying when you are full can be hard if you are used to undereating or overeating, or eating without thinking about eating, and therefore have lost touch with what real fullness feels like. You may need to slow down your eating and pay more attention to your body to notice when you start to feel full. If you are full, but have the impulse to keep on eating, put aside some of the food to eat when you get hungry later.

You may tend to eat more in social situations and when you are under stress. Or you may avoid eating in these same circumstances. Once you have identified events that cause you stress, you can find ways to relax. For example, before going to a party, imagine yourself at the event being calm, comfortable, and having a good time while eating moderately. After an intense meeting, sit quietly and do some deep breathing instead of wolfing down a candy bar.

You may prefer to skip meals and "save up" for a big lunch or dinner. However, skipped meals can lead to overeating later as well as making poor food choices due to excessive hunger. Try not to let yourself get too hungry.

If you eat for emotional nourishment, find other ways to nourish and nurture yourself. For example, after an argument, take a brisk walk or after a hard day work, soak in a hot bath to help soothe emotional rough edges. Reminding yourself that these negative feelings will pass can help you tolerate them.

There may be some food situations that are particularly difficult for you. Perhaps your best friend is a gourmet cook and is insulted when you don't eat everything she has prepared, or maybe your mother lovingly encourages you to eat more. Before you go to dinner, practice some gracious ways to say "No, thank you." Try a warm smile with a heartfelt, "This was a superb veal parmesan and I loved every bite! I can't possibly eat another morsel!" You will leave your hostess beaming, and you will feel better for not having gorged yourself.

Enjoy eating! It's fine to get pleasure from food, but be sure to find plenty of other sources of fun, too. Relying on food for excitement and pleasure can both rob you of seeking other ways to fill these needs and lead to misuse of food.

And don't forget to use the self-talk technique mentioned earlier. This is one of the most valuable techniques you can use in dieting. Just tell yourself, "I really do not need the large order of fries, the small ones will do. If I eat them I will fill really full and sick in my stomach." Tell yourself again the small order will be fine. Self-talk can give you the additional strength you need sometimes.

And remember to keep the following model in mind from the U.S. Department of Agriculture and the U.S. Department of Health and Human Services. The pyramid is an outline of what to eat each day. It's not a rigid prescription, but a general guide that lets you choose a healthful diet that's right for you. As you will notice, the pyramid calls for eating a variety of foods to get the nutrients you need and at the same time the right amount of calories to maintain a healthy weight.

FOOD GUIDE PYRAMID
A GUIDE TO DAILY FOOD CHOICES

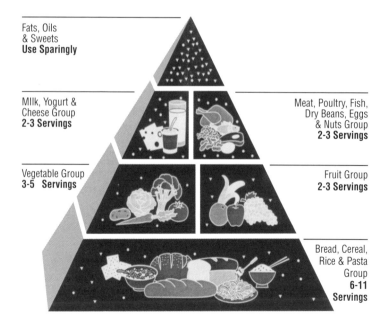

Fats, Oils
& Sweets
Use Sparingly

MIlk, Yogurt &
Cheese Group
2-3 Servings

Meat, Poultry, Fish,
Dry Beans, Eggs
& Nuts Group
2-3 Servings

Vegetable Group
3-5 Servings

Fruit Group
2-3 Servings

Bread, Cereal,
Rice & Pasta
Group
**6-11
Servings**

SOURCE: U.S. Department of Agriculture/U.S. Department of Health and Human Services

Make Exercise a Necessity

You may think of exercise as an unpleasant activity best left to those who are physically fit. Perhaps your own experiences with exercise have been uncomfortable and left you unwilling to repeat the effort. If you don't like your body and have unrealistic expectations about how you should look or how much you should exercise, it is bound to be unpleasant. On the other hand, exercise that is designed to fit your body type, comfort level, and lifestyle can help you feel good—not bad—about yourself.

I'm always amazed when my friends come to me for advice on losing weight. Of course, I mention the behavior modification plan spelled out in the previous pages and always add: "You must also exercise!" I usually hear a groan and then a litany of excuses for why they cannot exercise! Well, if you are not going to exercise, then good luck on trying to lose the weight and keeping it off.

Remember, exercising will not only help your physical appearance but your mental and emotional health as well!

Even small amounts of exercise can work and help you feel better about yourself. Begin by choosing a kind of exercise you think you would like. Then start small—perhaps a ten-minute walk around the block or the first five stretches on an exercise video. Be gentle with yourself and applaud yourself for whatever amount of exercise you do. If exercise has not been a part of your life before, check with your doctor before starting a new exercise program.

Experiment to find out what kinds of exercise you enjoy and what time of day you prefer to exercise. Perhaps riding a stationary bike while watching the evening news or using your lunch hour for a brisk midday walk will work best for you. With your doctor's approval, work toward a goal of doing twenty minutes or more, three times a week, of aerobic exercise (biking, brisk walking, or jogging).

Schedule your exercise times just as you would a business meeting or lunch with a friend, and keep these dates with yourself. After all, this is a commitment to exercising.

Look for opportunities to include natural exercise in your daily schedule. Park your car far enough away so that you have to walk a few extra steps, take the stairs up or down a floor rather than using the elevator, and walk those two blocks to the mailbox.

And remember, exercise doesn't have to be a fashion event. Wear loose comfortable clothes that let you move. Add music to the event. Wear your headphones or play the radio while exercising. It truly makes it much more enjoyable.

Take a look at this list of exercises and choose one, maybe two that you enjoy . . . and get started!

List of Exercises

Walking – The most common for those who want to lose weight—one you can do alone or with a buddy. It is highly aerobic; you can do this anywhere and it doesn't cost anything.

Jogging – This produces the fastest weight loss and can be done anywhere. So pop on the headphones and go for it! Just be safe and watch out for those ankle-biting dogs that like to sneak up on you.

Swimming – This form of exercise does not put much stress on your body and it is so refreshing.

Aerobic dance – This improves cardiovascular fitness and tones your muscles. A lot of women like it because of the group atmosphere and the motivational music. Or you can watch a tape or a class on the TV in the privacy of your own home.

Bicycling – You can use a regular two-wheeler or a stationary bike. This is a moderate aerobic activity.

Weight training – This, of course, will involve spending time at a gym.

Golf – A very enjoyable sport if you have the time and money. Walk the course for additional benefits.

Tennis – Another enjoyable activity; however, it will involve scheduling time for a court and money if you compete.

These are just a few ways to exercise that you may find enjoyable. Once you find an exercise you enjoy, stay with it. Exercise needs to be a lifelong commitment!

As I exited my daughters' elementary school one day, I saw a brightly colored sign with a great quote worth remembering:

Eat Right, Exercise Often, Be Healthy and
Feel Good About Yourself!

Chapter IV

Balancing Your Relationships

Are you beginning to see where this book is going? The goal is to make you happy and fulfilled in all areas of your life! Now let's take a look at your relationships so we can nourish those emotional and social needs so you can really feel good about yourself!

It seems all of life is relationships. We have relationships with everything. However, the most important relationship is with your spouse or significant other. During my graduate work one of my professors stressed that you must put your marital relationship before the children. Since I was expecting our first child, I thought to myself. . . "Gee, better remember that bit of information." Well, it is one you must remember and develop over the years or you might become that statistic we hear about so often— *one in two marriages ends in divorce.*

Research indicates that marital satisfaction declines when you have preschool-aged children. The fact is that some mothers tend to put their children before their husband. Let me give you an example.

After the birth of our first daughter, I was afraid to leave her with a sitter unless she was a nurse or my mother. Since my mother was seven hours away, she obviously was not an option. And nurses were unaffordable. So, I had the same excuse every time my husband would suggest going out: No mother, no money, no way!

This persisted for about six months until my neighbor with three children came over to have "the talk." She informed me that John had been complaining to her husband that I didn't want to go out and have fun anymore and that there was always an excuse. Well, Pam had it all planned. She arranged for two sitters, one just for our daughter, and the other for her kids. The neighborhood was having a get-together in the park (two blocks away from our house, a pay phone available, her husband had a beeper!). I could not find one excuse . . . had to go! Guess what? I went and had a wonderful time and realized I really missed being with my husband and friends.

How quickly I had forgotten what my professor had said. But the professor was right on target about the marital relationship. Make it the first priority in your life. Work on it, develop it and have fun with it!

Husband

To maintain a healthy satisfying relationship with your spouse, here are some suggestions to keep in mind:

- Plan a date every week! This could be dining out, a movie, having coffee or soda out, taking a walk or bike ride, or watching a favorite TV show together! Have it be your night—even if you don't go out, stress to the children that this is your night and that they are not to disturb! Children must learn to respect that parents need their own personal time together. If money is limited, have a parent watch your children or trade babysitting with another couple. A friend gives her sister and brother-in-law coupon books for Christmas, birthdays and anniversaries. It includes free babysitting hours and some overnights, too!

- Plan at least one weekend a year for a vacation together (no children included). Again, ask friends you feel comfortable leaving your children with (reci-procate this arrangement with your friends) or ask grandparents. During the time away, you may talk about the children—which you will do—but they may not go! And don't feel guilty about doing this—actually, they love the break from you, too! Even a local hotel will do for an overnight. If you can't afford it, stay home and turn your house into a romantic getaway and send the kids out to grandma's or to a friend's house!

So now I have you going out and developing that relationship. Did you know in today's society, on the average, couples only verbally communicate less than four minutes a day? I heard these statistics a few years ago and was astonished. No wonder divorce rates are so high. We have stopped talking verbally and nonverbally!

Let me give you a scenario of what I am trying to convey.

My husband had taken me out for my birthday to a favorite restaurant. I'm a people watcher and love to study nonverbal communication. I immediately noticed one married couple who were really, really communicating in many ways. She was looking into the eyes of her husband when she spoke to him, she was touching him by running her fingers over and around his shoulders and up his neck . . . and then she leaned over and laid a big kiss on his cheek! Let me tell you something, he was sitting there looking very proud. Now, they were communicating! And I bet I know exactly what the guy sitting across from them was thinking, "If only my wife would do that to me!"

Another couple were sitting in the booth to the side of me. They were barely communicating. She literally did not say one word until dessert. The entire time she was eating, she was looking down with a blank expression. Her husband would glance up at her as if he wanted to talk, but could not get her attention for the life of him. During dessert, she did, however, attempt to say a few words.

I thought to myself, "This is sad. Here, they got all dressed up and treated themselves to a nice dinner and they are apparently not even enjoying one another." She is very preoccupied with something or they have never learned how to talk to each other.

Now, don't think you have to be all over your husband like the first couple, but don't get like the second couple!

Let me give you a homework assignment. The next time you are with your husband, either on a date, a walk, in the car or anywhere out in public, show some affection toward him . . . hold his hand, give him a kiss, just do something! I guarantee he will enjoy it and other couples will take notice, too! And then tell him that you would like for him to try this experiment on you!

You need to work on your relationship. It's difficult sometimes with all our other commitments, which may include working, caring for the children, household responsibilities and that reoccurring PMS. But it can be a lot of fun, too. Here are some suggestions that have come from friends from all over the country.

- Send your husband notes, leave them in his car, tuck them in his briefcase or gym bag or coat pocket.

- Send him a thank-you note when he does something nice. We send everyone else one when they buy or do something nice for us.

- Surprise him with arranging for a sitter and have a date or night out!

- Leave him a fun or daring phone message! (Be careful what you say, in case someone intercepts the message.)

- Buy yourself some nice lingerie. Throw out the old and tattered stuff. My friend starts the new year off by buying all new panties and bras in January.

- Have a pet name for each other.

- Look nice for your husband when he comes through that door after a long day's work. You don't have to have your Sunday best on, but look decent. A friend once said, "I only have time to comb my hair twice a day . . . once in the morning and right before my husband comes home from work!"

- Give him a hug, kiss, or a pinch somewhere when he comes home from work. Tell him you missed him or ask how the meeting with so and so went. Don't start in about your bad day at work, with the kids, dog, etc. (save that for later).

- Have a box of cookies or flowers delivered to his place of work.

- Go on a picnic and pack his favorite drink with cheese and crackers!

- Back to the lingerie . . . some time include a piece in his briefcase or coat pocket or maybe his suitcase if he travels a lot. Believe me, your phone will be ringing when he discovers it!

- Have makeup on when your husband comes home (if you enjoy wearing it!). My mother would always excitedly rush to the bathroom around 4:00 in the afternoon and say, "Oh, your father is coming home so I'd better get my lipstick on!" I used to think this was silly, but now I know why she did it.

- Go dancing.

- Get away for a spiritual retreat for the weekend.

- Purchase tickets to a dinner theater, symphony or a Broadway musical.

- While your husband is showering in the morning, get him a cup of coffee or juice and have it waiting for him when he steps out of the shower or leave it with a cute note (i.e., good luck on your presentation or with your interview!).

- Write down ten things you like about your husband and give him the list.

- Encourage him to attend a few sporting events with his friends.

- Have a scavenger hunt! (No, I did not place this in the wrong chapter.) This is how it works and you can include the kids. Send your husband out to get something, and when he returns home have him find a note by following the clues. First clue, tell him to go to the mailbox. Then send him to the cleaner's to pick up the next clue, maybe to the pharmacy or card shop, for the next clue. Spread three or four clues around the area and then have him meet you at your favorite golden arches restaurant, etc., for breakfast, lunch, or dinner. You can do this for a "date" idea, too. Just arrange for a sitter to be at your house when he comes home from work. Have the sitter hand him the note and then provide clues that he must find you at your favorite restaurant or a hotel. Trust me, most men love this kind of thing!

- Surprise vacations are a hit, too. Plan a vacation from start to finish without your husband finding out. It may be driving him to a bed and breakfast or a hotel, or flying to another city for an overnight!

- Make his birthday special. Buy him a card, fix a favorite meal, or take him out to a restaurant he enjoys.

- Oh, and make Valentine's Day fun like you did when you were first married. Be creative here! (The nice lingerie, chocolates, candles . . .)

- And lastly, try never to go to sleep mad! Talk it out!

I honestly think if you try out some of these ideas on your husband you will see results. (Don't get discouraged if he doesn't respond immediately.) You and your husband will have a more loving and satisfying relationship. Hopefully, it will increase your intimacy, too. Men are physical beings and have a need to be sexually satisfied. Women have the same need, but intimacy also satisfies some of their emotional needs. However, women need attention and verbal communication as well to satisfy their emotional needs. So take time for communication and intimacy. You will both wake up smiling and have a much better day! I hope that your husband will realize that he needs to reciprocate the kindness and thank you for all you do for him and the children.

Also, if you are displaying kind acts toward your husband—talking to him, and giving him a hug or kiss everyday—you are modeling positive behaviors for your children to learn. Hopefully, they will carry this over into their future relationships.

I really value and remember the time and respect my parents put into their relationship. My father bragged about my mother, would show a lot of affection toward her, and take her on dates! I knew he really loved her. And I loved it when he would grab her and dance around the kitchen after a long day at work.

Likewise, my mother bragged about my father's hard work, his talents, would compliment his appearance, and on and on. This is the way it should be. Love your spouse, do nice things for him, brag about his qualities, and thank him for coming into your life. Hopefully, he will appreciate you more and together you will develop a long-term, loving relationship with opportunities for growth.

Friends

We also need to build and value our relationships with our friends. What is a friend? It is a person with whom you dare to be yourself. It is a person with whom you can pick up immediately where you left off the last time you were together—no matter how long ago. We all have friends like this and we need friendships like that!

We need to stay in touch with friends by phone or letters even if they live half way across the country. We need to make it a priority and find time to have lunch together or even a chat over a cup of coffee if they live close by.

My best friend from college lives in town, and we try to have lunch every three months. I always look forward to seeing Sara because I know we can talk about women's issues, be they serious or silly. I know I am honored and respected. We usually have a two-hour lunch filled with much laughter; she gives advice and I listen, I give advice and she listens, sometimes we cry, sometimes we laugh so hard we cry! All in all, we always leave each other saying, "I had so much fun," we will do it again soon. And we do!

If you have lost track of good friends, make it a priority to get back in touch. A group of us from all over the country decided to reunite for a weekend. Some of us had not seen each other for fifteen years. It was a weekend that we will never forget. We shared many joys. And we discussed the sorrowful times of losing a parent and the difficulties that are sometimes thrown at us during life's journey. But the climax of the weekend was the "tell-all" dinner conversation that sent us all into hysterical laughter! Needless to say, we had everyone's attention in the restaurant that night, including the owner's! I think every mom deserves a night out like this once in a while.

So call your friends, have them over for lunch, go to dinner, go to a movie, go window shopping, meet for coffee, go for a walk, send them a nice card to let them know how much you appreciate their friendship, remember their birthday and, most of all, don't be afraid to call them if you are in need of a listening ear or you have some joyous news to share.

Couple Friends

It is also important to have couple friends. Establish such relationships by dining out, having couples over for dinner, going on vacations or short trips, or just by enjoying mutual interests together. I must mention our friends the "Watsons" at this time. We met ten years ago while living in Oklahoma. At the time, we were young, childless and living on very limited budgets. However, we would get together on the weekends for potluck dinners and play the card game "spades."

I have never been a big game player of any kind. However, I have developed an interest as well as an appreciation for the game. It is easy to learn and is usually a quick game. However, the exciting part is the "fun" competitiveness between us and the silliness and laughter that is produced from this simple game.

Both families moved several times in the last ten years and many miles are now between us. However, we make it a priority to stay in touch and get together with our families at least once a year. And yes, we always find time to play at least one round of spades!

My friend Marie Thayer offered another great suggestion for enjoying your "couple friends." She plans an annual event with a theme. Her themes have included The Newlywed Game, a 60s night where everyone dresses up, scavenger hunt, and a mystery bus ride to a favorite place for dancing and dining! Be creative like her and have fun doing it!

We can all benefit from establishing these types of relationships and some will be lifelong! Here is a poem to sum up the essence of friends. My dear friend Shari Abrahamson Kyhl wrote this in a book that she gave me.

Having a friend like you
is learning this lesson of life
from the start . . .
That caring is sharing
that living is giving
that love is the key
to a happy heart!

Author unknown

Children

Our relationships with our children are also extremely important and long lasting. What do children really want from us, the grown-ups in their lives?

- They want to feel loved and valued.

- They want to feel as if they make a difference in our lives.

- They want to feel they are O.K. just the way they are.

- They want to feel we are proud of them, and don't wish they had been born to someone else.

Every child needs to know his or her parents feel this way in order to develop a healthy level of self-esteem and self-love.

Therefore, we need to make time and spend one-on-one time with each child. During this special time you need to look at your child, ask questions and listen. Really look, and listen. Don't be preoccupied with your own concerns. Have a date with your child. My friend labeled them this way: "Mommy-Son Date," "Mommy-Daughter Date," "Daddy-Son Date," "Daddy-Daughter Date." You need to make these times a very special opportunity to communicate. These dates will be very memorable for your children in years to come.

You can go to lunch at the child's favorite place (which is going to be inexpensive—we all know where they like to go), go to a park or go on a walk. Enjoy this time together, communicate and let your child know he or she can tell you anything and not be afraid to talk to you about any issue. Remember during these times to praise your child. Sometimes we only point out the negative behaviors. A friend of mine writes her children letters when they show kindness and helpfulness toward one another! This would be a great time to present such a note to your child. What a great way to reinforce and praise positive behaviors.

Don't forget to make their birthdays special! The minute the child wakes up on his special day, greet him with a "Happy Birthday" or sing the Happy Birthday song. Fix his favorite breakfast . . . give him a donut with a candle in it. Drop a note in her lunch box or back pack if she has to go off to school to let her know you will be thinking about her in a special way all day long.

Have some kind of party. Even if it just includes the immediate family.

Bake a cake and decorate it with lots of frosting and sprinkles, and don't forget the candles! Try trick candles, they are always a hit and will produce some big eyes and lots of giggles!!!!!

Here are some other suggestions for letting your children know they are very special to you.

- On Mother's Day, write a letter telling your child why she makes you feel like a special parent.

- Whenever your child gives you a gift, write a thank-you note and send it through the mail.

- Give compliments that relate to your child's personality, not just to accomplishments or physical appearance. For example, "You are really a good friend to Kendall," or "I thought you explained that really well."

- Let your child hear you pass on her opinion: "I thought those striped pillows might be too wild, but Rikki noticed how well they go with the wallpaper."

- On Saturday afternoon, explain that you're straightening the house for some special company. Prepare hors d'oeuvres or buy a prepared pie; make lemonade. Set out fancy paper plates and some games. Ask the kids to go out and ring the doorbell. Answer it and announce that they're the company.

- Call your son during a break from work and tell him you love him and can't wait to hear about his day when you arrive home.

- Once a day, say, "You're special," or "I love you" and give your daughter or son a big hug and a kiss on the cheek or on top of their head!

Remember to shower your children with love and attention, not material things. *Don't buy their love, show your love.* My sister-in-law, Rose, put it this way, "If you want your children to turn out well, spend twice as much time with them and half as much money on them."

I would like to end this chapter with a quote by former First Lady Barbara Bush from a graduation ceremony at an eastern college (appeared in the *Virginia-Pilot*, April, 1993).

> *She drew some of the crowd's most fervent applause when she said, "At the end of your life, you will never regret not having passed one more test, not winning one more verdict or not closing one more deal. You will regret time not spent with a husband, a friend, a child, or a parent."*

Chapter V

You Deserve a Break Some Days!

It had been a long six weeks in our household. It started before Christmas. Our daughter came down with the chicken pox, we had Christmas, we traveled, we came home, we had the flu, we had snow . . . lots of snow . . . then the sub-zero weather. Yes, you guessed it—the walls were closing in!

Since my husband would be home from work then, I thought to myself, "Just make it until Saturday, then you can get up, run and have a day off." Well, Saturday finally arrived. I crawled out of bed around 7:00. No one was up yet. "Great," I thought, "I'll take a run and release the stress." Well, I didn't check the weather forecast. I made it about a mile and thought to myself, "It is really cold out here!" I wondered where all the runners were. Instead of continuing, I decided to stop and shovel the sidewalk that had drifted overnight from the winds. I just wanted to be outside, away from everyone! About 8:00 life started to stir in our house. First, the kids all came bounding out of the house yelling, "Mommy, we want to help you." I looked up thinking, "Why me? Why do they somehow find me, no matter where I am?" Then my husband suddenly appeared saying, "Honey, I'm going to the fitness center to work out." I couldn't help myself. I screamed, and didn't care if I woke up the entire neighborhood, "You are going to take at least two of the kids!" He calmly replied, "I asked them, and no one wants to go with me." "But, you have to," I pleaded. "Sue, no one wants to go with me . . . Oh, by the way, I have to get the car serviced, too, so I'll see you around 11:00."

At this point, I was speechless, because I was crying and thinking, "I can't take this any more!" However, I quickly realized that if I cried too much more, my tears were going to freeze on my face. So, I pulled myself together and decided to confront what awaited me inside those four walls. To my surprise, the morning turned out to be very productive.

The children played well together and I accomplished a lot around the house. (I think John prompted them and begged them to be good for their mother.) When my husband returned home later that morning, he thanked me for letting him go and then told me the afternoon was all mine! And enjoy I did!

Have you been there? I think we all have experienced something similar to this scenario. We need to take a break sometimes and go and do something enjoyable for ourselves. This pertains to all mothers—whether they stay at home or work. A lot of my friends who work say they feel guilty taking any more time away from their kids. Don't feel guilty; you need some personal time, too! Everyone does, no matter what they do.

All Kinds of Ideas for Giving Yourself a Break

So what are the ways you, as a mother, treat yourself? I've talked to some women who do a really good job of treating themselves and then there are those who need some help and guidance. I'm going to provide you with a variety of ideas to treat yourself! Here they are; some are free and some have a cost attached.

- Enjoy a free makeup consultation (any cosmetic counter will provide this for you).

- Have a massage.

- Call a friend or family member to chat.

- Treat yourself to a manicure or pedicure.

- Enjoy yourself at a day spa.

- Go shopping or just window shopping.

- Have lunch with a friend.

- Drive around the block by yourself.

- Drive to a scenic neighborhood and take a walk.

- Get a facial.

- Enjoy a soda and sandwich and the peace and quiet by yourself.

- Exercise at a health club.

- Read the paper in a park.

- Plan a walk with a friend or by oneself, or take the dog.

- See a movie; rent a new release or an old favorite video.

- Visit an art gallery.

- Light a candle and enjoy cooking dinner.

- Go hunting for antiques.

- Take an historical walking tour.

- Visit garage sales and estate sales.

- Work a crossword puzzle.

- Go away for a weekend or overnight with girlfriends.

- Read a good novel or magazine. Utilize the resources in your public library.

- Browse in a book store.

- Go for a good run.

- Sit on the beach and relax.

- Paint your fingernails and toenails.

- Take a bike ride.

- Read a daily devotional book, Upper Rooms, etc.

- Run errands by yourself.

- Crank up the music and dance.

- Have coffee at a quiet, quaint coffee shop (read or write letters there).

- Go to a concert or play. Take advantage of productions that are free to the public.

- Attend a holiday open house.

- Enjoy a Girls' Night-Out.

- Take a bubble bath. Light some candles, listen to music or read, or just take a bath and relax!

- Hire a cleaning service at times, if affordable.

- Go to an art museum.

- Start a supper club with friends.

- Visit a botanical garden.

- Have time alone in your own house.

Developing Special Interests and Talents

Don't forget to enjoy and develop your interests, too, when you have a break.

Many of the interests mentioned below will stimulate your mind and provide the mental nourishment that we all need. Of course, how we get to enjoy some of our interests will depend on the timing in your life. For instance, if you just had your third baby, you will probably find it difficult to get very involved in a societal concern that takes time away from the home or workplace. So, you might realize you'd better put it on hold until you feel organized enough to start back on the project. Or if this is your first baby, you may just need time to adjust to this major transition in your life. Whatever the case, you will get your life back and when you do, you need to focus some of your energy on yourself! Remember that each one of us has special talents and abilities. So use them!

- Play or take up the piano or any musical instrument.
- Study birds and take up watching them.
- Go horseback riding.
- Learn to play golf.
- Take up roller blading, ice skating, or roller skating.
- Try bowling; join a league.
- Enjoy gardening. Plant a garden or join a garden club.
- Take an art class.
- Take a pottery class.
- Enjoy crafts.
- Play softball, tennis, volleyball, or swimming. Try water aerobics.
- Take up knitting, cross-stitch or quilting.
- Try a scuba diving class.
- Read motivational and self-help books.

- Pick a decorating project for your home and follow it through from start to finish.

- Call an older adult on a weekly basis. It is amazing the history you will learn, and the wisdom you'll gain.

- Enroll in a cooking class.

- Take an adult education class (i.e., investment class, yoga, interior design, writing class, etc.). These normally last two or three sessions and are inexpensive. Call your local junior college or school system for a listing.

- Join a church choir and sing away. Pastor Bob once said, "Singing is good for the soul!"

- Pick a societal concern and get involved.

- Get involved in the cultural arts, symphony, etc.

- Volunteer your services at places that: feed or give shelter to the homeless

  — support those afflicted with AIDS

  — help battered women or abused children

  — work with the disabled

  — work with the elderly, dying, nursing homes, assisted living centers, retirement centers, etc.

- Volunteer your time to help at the American Heart Association, Cancer Society, Alzheimer Association, National Kidney Foundation, etc. These organizations have many volunteer activities. Check your local yellow pages for many of these type organizations.

- Take a photography class; become a photographer.

- Take a floral design course to learn to make arrangements and wreaths—for yourself or for gifts.

- Get involved in your church. Share your abilities and talents by joining committees, teaching Sunday School, leading youth groups, belonging to the women's group.

- Attend a church or synagogue, but involve yourself so you will meet people and develop your support system.

- Visit an elderly person in a retirement or nursing home each week.

- Join a book club or start one!

- Join a bunco group or bridge group.

- Take voice lessons and then try karaoke.

- Take karate or any self-defense class.

- Check what classes and activities the local YMCA or YWCA offers.

- Hospitals provide a variety of classes for women. Call the women's resource center and get a listing. Some are free, too! (Hospitals usually have good support groups for new mothers.)

- Start sewing! Make simple Halloween costumes or outfits for the kids.

- Take an aerobics class or start one with friends and hire a college student to watch the children.

- Join a Bible study group.

- Learn a foreign language.

- Try new recipes.

- Research a business idea.

- Refinish furniture or paint it.

- Get involved with local, state or national politics. Pick a cause and fight for it!

- Volunteer to conduct tours of historic sites and museums.

- Staff a cancer, rape-crisis, domestic abuse, or child abuse hot line.

- Write a book, poetry, journal articles. Buy a *Writer's Market Guide* and get published.

- Read the opinion section of your local newspaper and submit a letter to the editor.

- Join an investment club or find out how to start one.

- Get involved in PEO (an educational sorority that provides scholarships to young women and other forms of support).

- Get involved in your college sorority in the area in which you live.

- Join Beta Sigma Phi Sorority, a national service oriented and support group for women.

- Get involved in Child Care Action Campaign (NY, NY) An advocacy group for quality child care for all children.

Making Extra Cash

Why not start a home business? The following are some ways to make some extra cash. Before you start, make sure you research your idea carefully. Do your homework. Develop a marketing plan and be prepared to work hard. Check licensing and tax laws, as well as insurance needs.

The following books are helpful references for starting a home business: *Mompreneuers: A Mother's Practical Step-by-Step Guide to Work-at-Home Success* by Patricia Cobe and Ellen H. Parlapiano and *The Stay at Home Mom's Guide to Making Money* by Liz Folger.

To get you thinking, consider these lines of business:

- Graphic art design—freelance

- Floral arranging—wreaths, arrangements, etc.

- Makeup consultant (Jafra, Avon, Mary Kay, etc.)

- Toy consultant (Discovery Toys)

- Kids clothing (Kelly Kids, etc.)

- Creative Memories or Photographs and Memories—promote and sell products to preserve and decorate your photo albums

- Selling baskets for Longerberger Baskets

- Commercial cleaning of offices, stores and restaurants

- Housecleaning

- Baking and selling cookies, cakes or breads to bakeries or coffee shops

- The Pampered Chef (kitchen shows to demonstrate use of kitchen tools, stoneware, and cookware)

- Teaching piano

- Tutoring children in math, algebra or calculus if you have the expertise; call your local schools to get contacts

- Personal fitness trainer

- Aerobics instructor

- Word processing service for college students and job seekers

- Accounting business

- Professional organizers—organize closets, kitchens, offices

- Specialty market—recipe salad dressings, salsas, barbecue sauces, pastas, etc.

- Desktop publishing—medical billing or transcription

- Organizing and assisting the elderly (Do this only if you enjoy older adults.)

- Children's van services to arts, music programs, daycares, etc.

- Books, CD-ROMs, other educational items, such as supplements to school or aimed at home-schooling families

- Catering parties (adult or children parties)
- Video children's school programs and sell the tapes to the parents
- In-home chef
- Personal gift baskets for corporations or individuals
- Childcare—do this in your home because you love children and not because you just need the money!

Attend Chamber of Commerce meetings and join professional women's groups in your local area to promote your business.

Other Kinds of Support

Lastly, find support from others. Ask your husband, find a good sitter, babysitting co-op, preschool, daycare, or trade with friends or family members so you can have that much deserved break. I have been truly blessed in this area. Everyone should have a Mrs. Plumb as a babysitter. When she opens the door, she is always smiling and greets my child wholeheartedly. The preschool where my older daughter goes gives me the same feeling—everyone is always smiling and so positive. I know they will protect, nurture and love my child while she is in their care.

Everyone should have a babysitter, preschool or daycare that does this! Every mother needs to have this same reassuring feeling every time she drops her precious child off somewhere. You must find someone you trust and feel comfortable leaving your child with so that you can really enjoy your break.

Let's take a look at some other ways to find social support for ourselves.

Support from Others and Groups!

Do we ever need support from others when we have young children!

Personally, I think our country could do a better job in helping others in need!

Husband

Let's start with getting help and support from your husband, or if you are divorced from your ex-husband. Some husbands or ex's are good about anticipating and offering a helping hand at the appropriate time. But if your husband or ex needs to be told when to help, then tell him! When I began working, I thought I could do it all. I quickly realized I needed to divvy up the responsibilities with the father of those girls. But I quickly slipped into doing everything for everyone once I started staying home again. It wasn't long before I began to resent it!

So, now every Sunday evening we go over our schedules for the week. We talk about who needs to help with what so we have a fairly clear picture of everyone's week and needs. For example, I tell John when he needs to watch the kids, help with baths or tuck the girls in bed. And it can change. Sometimes if I have had a very long stressful day, I just tell him he needs to take over for the evening.

Of course, you can be totally organized like our friends the Chambons. Their large weekly duty chart includes such a detailed list that no one could get confused about who is to do what in that household!

Parents, Family Members or Friends

Parents, family members and friends are the next link in the support system. Utilize these people as much as possible to help raise your children. Single mothers especially need some backup support from friends and family. Unfortunately, the majority of us today do not have parents or siblings living close by.

Grandparents can be wonderful support. They also can pass on knowledge and wisdom to their grandchildren. And they usually have an abundance of patience and love to share. My mother-in-law, Helen, has always been great about taking one grandchild at a time for a week in the summer. She spends quality time with the children during this special week. I remember my grandmother "Mammy" always spending special time with her grandchildren. Those are memories that I will cherish as long as I live.

So if you have family and friends to lean on for help, do so. But don't take advantage of their help or come to expect it!

Neighbors

Some neighborhoods are great at the "art of neighboring." I grew up in a community where neighbors were very helpful at the time of a birth of a baby, illness of a child or parent or the death of a loved one. They were there offering support to help with children, prepare a meal or grocery shop.

We have moved several times and lived in three different neighborhoods. The neighbors were great when our first daughter was born, preparing meals and offering support. However, I remember vividly being very overwhelmed after the birth of our third daughter, lonely and isolated in a new area, worried over our middle daughter's lame leg, and depressed over my father's recent diagnosis of cancer.

During that time, I had support that I was very grateful for, too. I received support from praying to God to give me strength and patience to make it through the day. I received support from a caring husband. When he arrived home, I was bolting out the door after dinner, to take a walk, drive around by myself in the car to listen to music, or go to the local grocery store to browse through magazines.

I also had support from my best friend, Sara, who works full-time, but would call me weekly to chat. And I had support from a gracious lady who lived in the neighborhood. She took my two older children to preschool almost every day for six months. She prepared a delicious meal and invited the girls over for lunch. One day I asked Leslie Oliver, a mother of three herself, "How could I ever repay you for helping me?" Her reply was one I will never forget. "Just help another mom in need some day!" Again, thank you, Leslie, for your support during one of the most difficult and painful times in my life!

So now I try to repay Leslie by helping other mothers. I offer to carpool, take children for the day, prepare meals or organize other neighbors to take meals! When I hear about someone in need, I try to help in any way possible.

My current support system is great. My new neighbor, Dorinda, is one of those who are good at anticipating. She is always one step ahead, offering to watch one or all of my children depending on my needs. I try to reciprocate her generosity and thoughtfulness.

My neighbors, Terri and Jackie, and I have worked out a great support system. They both work full-time and I'm currently staying home. I told them I want to be their backup if they need me and I'm available. I can watch their children before or after school since I am home anyway, or if they have an unexpected meeting come up. I also told them to list me as an emergency contact with school, sitters, etc., too. To reciprocate, they often take my children after they get home from work and on the weekends. Working mothers, single mothers and stay-at-home mothers need their neighbors for support at times. And I strongly believe we should be there for each other and for our children.

If you know women going through a divorce or who are single, please offer your support. Surprise them with a meal, offer to take their children for an evening so they can have some quiet time or enjoy an interest. Send your teen over to babysit for a few hours for free!

I think this is where we can unite working mothers and stay-at-home mothers. Do not judge or voice your opinion about their choices. Instead, determine each other's needs, support each other and lend a helping hand. That's what neighbors are for!

Church

Churches or synagogues can be wonderful sources of support to women who have small children or who have recently relocated. Most churches or synagogues offer a variety of programs mothers and their children can get involved in. Some even provide special support groups for all moms with young children. These programs may be affiliated with a national group such as MOPS (Mothers of Preschoolers) or be self-organized.

Involve yourself in committee work, teach Sunday School, or sing in the choir. This also provides you a way to meet other mothers. And notify them when you've had a baby or an illness in the family. Most likely, they will provide meals or help with the other children during this time of need.

Support Groups

There are other support groups you can involve yourself in. In your local area check the hospitals, women resource centers and ask for a listing of classes. Calling community centers, YMCAs, YWCAs, or check the newspaper listing for different support groups.

Here are some national support groups that are of great benefit to many mothers in our country.

F.E.M.A.L.E.

F.E.M.A.L.E. (Formerly Employed Mothers At the Leading Edge) is a non-profit organization for women who have left the full-time workforce to raise children at home. It is an organization for all women dealing with the transition between paid employment and at-home motherhood. It is NOT about opposing mothers who work outside the home. F.E.M.A.L.E. is about respecting, supporting and advocating for choice in how one combines working and parenting.

F.E.M.A.L.E. was created as a support group for women who have interrupted their careers to raise their families and as an advocacy group for employment and family issues. Both purposes—support and advocacy— are important in promoting the needs and interests of at-home mothers, and, in fact, all parents striving to do their best for their families, their work and themselves.

Regardless of how women come to the decision to stay home or what they did in their former lives, they grapple with most of the same emotions and reactions in going from paid work to at-home work. Many experience a loss of identity, self-esteem, direction, feedback, and structure and find a need to redefine their roles in familial and marital relationship. F.E.M.A.L.E. assists in addressing these issues through involvement in local chapters and articles in the newsletter, *Female Forum.*

Catherine Carbone Rogers, an active member, describes F.E.M.A.L.E. as a wonderful resource for women who find themselves dealing with the transition from full-time employment to raising children at home.

F.E.M.A.L.E. provides the opportunity to get together regularly with other women in the same stage in life and the same "line of work"—raising children. It allows women to get a break from their responsibilities at home a couple of evenings a month. Monthly meetings most often involve discussion of some topic of interest to our members—not necessarily a parenting topic. In fact, we avoid spending too much time on parenting issues and strive for a balanced slate of topics so that we are nurturing the whole woman, not just the mother.

To find out if a chapter exists in your area or to inquire about starting a group, contact F.E.M.A.L.E. at the following address:

F.E.M.A.L.E.
National Headquarters
P.O. Box 31
Elmhurst, Illinois 60126

MOMS CLUB

"The MOMS Club has given me the opportunity to meet other stay-at-home moms in my area and share with each other the trials and triumphs of motherhood."

Shelli Sarandos, President, MOMS Club
of Glendale-Arrowhead Ranch, Arizona

The MOMS Club is a support group just for you, the mother-at-home of today, interested in the world around you, wanting a variety of activities for you and your children and proud of your choice of at-home mothering for your family!

Nationally, the MOMS Club has hundreds of chapters across the country and 18,000 plus members! It is a great support group for all at-home mothers.

The MOMS Club sponsors Activity Groups for members with common interests. These change as interests change, but include activities such as children's playgroups, gourmet lunch groups, arts n'crafts, coupon exchanges, a monthly MOMS Night Out and babysitting coops, among others.

For more information or to see if a MOMS Club exists in your area please contact:

MOMS Club
25371 Rye Canyon Rd.
Valencia, CA 91355

MOPS

Dear Friend,

I am very concerned about the isolation of mothers of small children. I know how desperately a ministry like MOPS is needed today!

Dr. James Dobson, Author, Psychologist
Focus on the Family

Do you know the women he is talking about?

Perhaps you've seen her at the store with the newborn in her arms and the two-year-old tugging on her leg.

She may be new in your community with no friends, no family close by.

She knows that mothering is an important job, but at times all she feels is overwhelmed, fatigued, alone, or lost.

She could be your neighbor, daughter, friend. She could be you.

Elisa Morgan, President

MOPS (Mothers of Preschoolers) is a program designed for mothers with children under school age, infant through kindergarten. Mothers, not all the same age, but all in the same phase of life. Women . . . different sizes, different colors, different lifestyles, some from the church, many unchurched . . . but all with similar needs and a shared desire—to be the very best mothers they can be!

The goal of MOPS is to nurture all mothers of preschoolers, to reach out with encouragement, evangelism, and effective leadership opportunities. MOPS offers a haven for frazzled nerves; an encouraging, accepting atmosphere where a mom finds out she's not alone; a quality children's program, MOPPETS, where her little ones are loved and encouraged. The MOPS group provides encouragement, support, teaching, and friendships in a relaxed atmosphere of caring, sharing and fun. In these relationships moms find answers for their simple, everyday dilemmas and discover a safe place to explore and discuss life's situations. MOPS helps moms . . . and MOPS makes a difference in the lives of their families.

MOPS believes in mentoring: MOPS believes in older, more experienced women helping younger women to love their families and to grow personally. This is an important part of the MOPS program. Mentors share, based on their own experience and wisdom, about practical, meaningful ways to fulfill the varied roles of mother, wife, and woman. The teaching is rooted in Biblical truth and brought to life through the caring concern of the older woman who remembers what she needed during this time of life. The young women learn, some for the first time, that Biblical principles are a practical and relevant guide for everyday living.

Following the teaching time, the mothers break into discussion groups to discuss the topics more personally. The intimate, safe, accepting atmosphere of these groups, led by the mothers themselves, allows women to express their thoughts and feelings, sharing their frustrations, successes, and experiences. They find out that they are not alone, that what they are doing does make a difference, and lifelong friendships are made.

At MOPS, women have the opportunity to be creative during a time of crafts and creative activity. Each woman feels a great sense of accomplishment as she completes an activity, something she would probably not have the time or energy to attempt at home. This time not only builds self-confidence in mothers, it is also a lot of fun!

If you would like to join or start a MOPS program in your area, contact:

MOPS International, Inc.
1311 South Clarkson Street
Denver, Colorado 80210
303-733-5353

Mother-to-Mother Ministry

Most mothers (no matter what their circumstances) have the same hopes and dreams for their children.

Mother-to-Mother Ministry is an ecumenical, volunteer program that brings together women of adequate income and mothers with low income for the purpose of increasing and understanding across the lines of income, culture, race, age, education and religion. The program offers personal friendship and emotional support to women who are usually single, have limited resources and are responsible for raising a family.

Two to four women form a team. They visit each other and exchange ideas, working to build their friendship and trust. Together they identify areas of concern, set goals and work to achieve them. A local coordinator recruits and matches team volunteers. "We are here to help a mother discover her own strength, not to rescue her," as quoted by a support mother.

Mother-to-Mother Ministry makes a significant contribution in helping prevent child abuse and neglect, and in giving positive feedback and reinforcement to disadvantaged mothers and their children.

The goals of this program are as follows:

- Participants become whole persons and grow to their greatest potential.

- Injustices are recognized and the cycle of poverty is broken.

- Volunteers become more sensitive to the needs and difficulties of low-income and minority persons.

To find out if there is a program in your community, contact the program coordinator and indicate your willingness to become involved. If there is no program serving your area, talk to your friends and pastor about organizing a group.

Contact the national coordinating office:

Mother-to-Mother Ministry
Homeland Industries
Christian Church (Disciples of Christ)
P.O. Box 1986
Indianapolis, Indiana 46206-1986
317-635-3100

National Organization of Mothers of Twins Clubs (NOMOTC)

The National Organization of Mothers of Twins Clubs, Inc. (NOMOTC) was founded in 1960 for the purpose of promoting the special aspects of child development that relate specifically to multiple-birth children.

NOMOTC is a network of local clubs representing individual parents of multiples—twins, triplets and quadruplets. The goal is to improve public awareness of the needs of multiple-birth children by fostering the development of local support groups, enhancing the quality of educational materials available to parents, educators and others and by cooperating with and participating in research projects that involve multiples and/or their families.

NOMOTC promotes the concept of mutual support for parents of multiples. Opportunities for self-help and emotional support are provided through local and statewide meetings. The membership department operates a support service program to assist individuals in special situations. These services include Pen Pals for parents whose multiples have disabilities or for parents who have disabilities affecting their childrearing abilities; bereavement support for those who have experienced the loss of multiple birth children; and single parent outreach.

For more information or to find a support group in your area, contact:

> NOMOTC
> P.O. Box 23188
> Albuquerque, New Mexico 87192-1188
> 505-275-0955 (Executive Office)
> 1-800-243-2276 (Club Referrals Only)

Reminder

Find the support you need during this time in your life. There are lots of possibilities. I challenge you to treat yourself and develop your interests! Enjoy your life to the fullest—you deserve it!

> *Do not wait until tomorrow to do what you mean to do today. Live each day as if it is the only one you have. Live your life rather than simply pass through it. It is never too late to start living and growing!*
>
> Elisabeth Kubler-Ross

SECTION TWO

Dealing with

Your Children

Chapter VI

Will This Day Ever End?

How many times have you said that? Or at least thought it? There have been many days over the past eight years when this thought has crossed my mind. My husband usually knows it has been a particularly long and even a bad day when he comes home and sees me scanning the want ads because I cannot take playing "Duck, Duck, Goose" one more time! Working mothers feel the same way sometimes, when they've worked all day and come home to the second part of the day, which can be pretty stressful and long at times. I remember those working days, too!

A friend, Diane Trimble, made an honest comment to me one day. She said, "Sue, I have both worked and stayed home. And believe me, staying home with children is so much harder!" I think this statement is true for many, given I have also done both. However, I personally find it is the "parenting" that can be the most trying and difficult some days for all mothers. There's just more of it when you stay home all day.

For the most part, the week days and weekends go by fairly quickly since you are busy with your schedule and your children's schedules. But what do you do on those days that seem to drag on forever and be so monotonous? Let me fill your head with lots of great ideas collected from resources, other mothers, and my own experience.

A basic suggestion is that you and the kids get out of the house every day even if you just run errands. You need to get fresh air, let the sunshine beat down on your face, and see other people—even if it is just the checkout clerk at the grocery. They are normally very talkative and smiling! This is a recommendation to help your mental health.

Another suggestion is that if you can't go out because the kids are sick, etc., open up all your drapes, turn on the lights and play music. This will also help your state of mind during those sick, gloomy winter or rainy days!

Let me make an important point here. Do not feel as though you need to entertain your children all day. They must be able to think for themselves and play on their own. Suggest creative play. Don't place them in front of a TV or let them play video games all day long. Instead, suggest playing school, house, dress up, coloring, puzzles or having fun in the sandbox!

Creative Ideas for "Shortening the Day"

Here is a list of ideas for those long days—these can be rainy days, winter days, summer days, sick days or even occasional "normal" days. Utilize any of these ideas with your children where you see appropriate.

- Invite a playmate over. Have your child plan activities for his or her friend. Sometimes it helps to have a friend over to divert your child's attention.

- Always have a craft box ready with ample supplies: playdough, paper, paint, markers, crayons, glue, cotton balls, macaroni—anything that helps your child be creative.

- Let them pretend they are mixing up a recipe. Give them water, flour and spices you never use. Give them a bowl and spoon—watch them have fun!

- Sponsor a "Happy Hour" on Fridays from 4-6 p.m. for moms and children. Supply drinks and snacks for everyone or ask others to help out. Fill the wagon with ice and stock it with juice packs for the kiddos!

- Search for indoor treasures. Hide things around the house. Give them a map and flashlight and tell them to enjoy the search!

- Attend story time at local libraries and bookstores.

- Bake and decorate cookies and cupcakes.

- Take the children to the fire station or to a nursing home.

- Fix a sack lunch and have a picnic indoors!

- Go to the public library and check out books.

- Go for a car ride.

- Play board games.

- Make get-well cards for a sick neighbor or nursing home residents.

- Plan and make a meal for an elderly or sick neighbor.

- Have a beach party in the middle of winter. Let the children put their swimming suits on and fill the tub with warm water.

- Look at family photo albums and tell your children stories about when they were babies, one-year-olds, etc.

- Watch family videos from birth to present.

- Make collages from magazines and cut, cut, cut!

- Go bug hunting! Don't forget the container!

- Go to a park.

- Go to a pet store and look at the animals.

- Go to a fast food restaurant and enjoy a break from cooking.

- Make a tent or hiding place for the kids.

- Have a puppet show.

- Read lots of books.

- Play restaurant—take orders and serve toy food!

- Have a tea party.

- Take a "field trip" to a local fish market or super market and see the live lobsters and all the different types of fish. Talk about which ones live in your area, which ones live up North or down South.

- Make a new craft project—inexpensive ones like magic pen pictures, sand art, or fuse beads.

- Take a long walk, pick up sticks, rocks, leaves, etc.

- String necklaces using cereal.

- Have a dress-up parade.

- Make potato art, cut a potato in half, give them paint and paper and let them make a design.

- Make masks out of paper sacks.

- Go to the bakery or donut shop for a special treat!

- Attend sports clinics and camps during holiday breaks and summer vacation.

- Buy a kite and head to a park, beach or an open field.

- Make a leaf picture by taking two pieces of wax paper, gluing leaves on one and pasting the edges of the other for a cover.

- Make a bird feeder. Use a toilet paper holder, spread peanut butter on it, sprinkle it with bird seeds and use yarn to hang it.

- Paint pictures in the snow. Fill spray bottles with water and food coloring and use the mixture to paint snowmen, draw pictures, or make crazy designs in the snow.

- Use sidewalk chalk; make a hopscotch grid.

- Arrange an art show for the neighborhood kids. Invite children to bring a drawing board or use the driveway. Have them paint a picture and invite the moms or older siblings to buy the kids' pictures for a nominal fee.

- Let the kids run through a sprinkler or spray them with a water hose.

- Let the children help plant a flower or vegetable garden.

- Go to the swimming pool.

- Give the kids a bucket of water and clean paint brush and let them paint the house or driveway. Discuss what happens to their "paint."

- Play a game of "Go Fish." Use two cards for each number 1-10. Let the children match numbers. You can make your own cards or use a regular deck of cards.

- Play "bigger" or "smaller." Name an object and have the children find something bigger and then something smaller. This game can be played outside or in the house.

- Make paper towel placemats. Let children trace around a plate, fork, knife, spoon and glass. Let them set the table using their placemats as a guide.

- Make a punching bag. Stuff an old pillow case with shredded newspaper.

- Try this recipe for play dough. Mix 1 cup flour, 1 cup water, 1/2 cup salt, 2 tablespoons vegetable oil, and 2 tablespoons cream of tartar. Add a couple of drops of food coloring. Cook, stirring constantly until dough pulls away from the side of pot. Remove from pot and knead until smooth. Add flour if sticky. A few drops of peppermint extract makes the playdough smell delicious.

When you are cooped up for several days, the kids need to release some energy. Here are five-minute indoor energy outlets:

Hallway Races

- Time sprints down the hall using string or crepe paper for the finish line.

- Hold one-legged, hopping, or pillowcase "sack" races.

- Have kids long roll down the hall, with arms and legs straight at their sides.

I'm a Statue

- You or a child call out the names of objects or animals, which everyone imitates; hold the position or imitate the animal for thirty seconds.

- In a room with floor space, have kids spin around a few seconds, then fall down and hold the position they fall in for ten counted seconds.

Living Room/Hallway Obstacle Course

- Push furniture to the edges of the room, or use a long hall. Find boxes to jump in, pillows to bounce on, towels in a circle to step in (like tires), and a stack of books to jump over. Time everyone running through the obstacle course several times.

Marathon Dancing

- Ask everyone to name their favorite fast-paced song. Get the furniture out of the way, put the music on, and give in to a few minutes of dancing fever!

Other Reasons Why the Day May Seem Endless

Of course you're a busy adult. But that's not the only reason why playing with your preschool-aged child can be so exhausting. Here are some other, subtler reasons for your fatigue.

You're tired because you feel guilty. Guilt is an exhausting emotion. When you don't feel like playing with your child, but think you *should*, you place a heavy load on yourself, a load that often produces bone-wearying fatigue.

How many parents feel exactly as you do? Let's put it this way: The feeling is as common as breathing. So quit blaming yourself; you'll be amazed how much energy that frees up.

You're bored. If you have to play "Candyland" or "Baby" one more time, you think you'll go out of your mind. But *boring* is another word for *tiresome*. It's a short trip from there to *tired-making*. And tired-making situations kill fun, thereby defeating the purpose of playing with your child in the first place.

So what can you do the next time you find yourself bored to tears with one of your child's favorite games? One tactic is to divert him, channel his energy into something both of you find interesting. For example, if you find board games a bore, try using the play surface as a springboard to imaginative play. Ask your child, "What would life be like in a *real* Candyland?" or "What would the people who lived on Gumdrop Mountain, or in the Molasses Marsh, look like?" Make up stories with your youngster about these places on the board, or invent new characters together. A little imagination can bring a whole new dimension to a worn-out activity.

If you just can't escape from a game that bores you, try something else: Change the focus of your attention. Play and pay attention, but put more energy into *watching* your child. It can be a joy to note that your four-year-old's construction-paper creatures now include not only monsters, but recognizable animals and people; or that your five-year-old's "teacher" in the game of "school" is now more believably teacherish.

You're preoccupied. If you're thinking about work while you're supposed to be helping your daughter build a block castle, not only will you be bored, but your child will sense your absence as well, and the activity will turn out to be a dud.

What's your alternative? "Try letting go of your adult agenda," says Virginia Casper, Ph.D., developmental psychologist and professor at the Bank Street Graduate School. "If you can do it, you will find it pays off in surprising ways."

All the things you put off will need doing later, of course. But being willing to lay them aside gains you admission to a world from which adults are generally excluded: The realm of true play, of the absolute, time-less, completely pleasurable kind of play that you probably haven't experienced since your own childhood. Only now it's even better:

Your child is your playmate.

So, when you do have one of those long days, remember this quote from Rhonda Restivo (mother of three children).

> *There is a light at the end of the tunnel. Before you know it, they will be going off to grade school and then it is suddenly time to take them off to college! So, tell yourself they are only young for a short time! Enjoy them and love them!*

Chapter VII

Please Don't Whine, Scream or Fight Today!

It was Mother's Day! The day every mother looks forward to with great excitement! My special day in 1994 started with a wake-up call and a delicious breakfast prepared and served to me in bed by my children. Then I had the honor of being escorted to church with my husband and three cheerful daughters. After church we headed for my favorite restaurant for brunch. The last stop was at the nursery to purchase flowers for planting in the afternoon, which has become a family tradition every year.

What a great day it had turned out to be. The children had displayed their best behavior. They had all joined in the fun of planting the flowers. It was not only an enjoyable day, it was productive as well. I felt so proud to be their mother.

One thing I really wanted to do was to watch the Judd television special later in the evening. This was something I had been looking forward to all week long . . . what more wonderful a way to end this memorable day than to watch this program by myself in peace and quiet. So we bathed the children early with the goal of having them all tucked in bed before 7:50 p.m. Ten minutes before showtime!

Well, the mission was accomplished. The girls were all nestled away. My last words to them were "I love you, and remember, I don't want to hear anything out of you because mommy has a show she really wants to watch." (Unfortunate use of words here; instead, I should have given them a choice before I left the room . . . I'll explain later.)

I had just settled into my big easy chair, when I detected some whining coming from the children's bedroom. I reassured myself, thinking, "Oh they'll stop, surely they do not want to ruin mommy's day." Then, another daughter screams—one yelling that the other was singing so loud than she couldn't get to sleep, the other that she needed a drink and a cheese stick. Then the most commonly spoken word around the house was uttered . . . "Mommy!!!"

Remaining positive and in control, thinking . . . well the show hasn't really started yet, just a bunch of commercials . . . I proceeded upstairs and calmly said, "Girls, I do not want to hear any more out of you. If I have to come back up here, you will all be in big trouble." (Again, wrong choice of words; it sounded like a threat using fighting words, which never works . . . I'll explain the way I should have handled it later on.)

I barely hit the landing when they were at it again; this time screaming and verbally fighting. Well, I had had it! I went stomping up the steps like a raging bull and started screaming at the top of my lungs. It went something like this . . . "Girls, I cannot and will not take this anymore (I was pounding my fist on the bed—screeching by now), I told you I wanted to watch that show." I was just about to threaten spanking when I noticed the bedroom window was wide open! I mean open all the way! I stopped screaming immediately because at that point I saw every neighbor imaginable in their backyards with their eyes focused on the Dawes' house. Instead, I turned around and exited the room, red faced, filled with embarrassment and wondering, "How will I ever face them again?" I proceeded down the stairs to the basement where I found my husband diligently preparing his agenda for the next day at work. I let him have it for opening all the windows and not telling me.

Who was out of control here? Who handled the situation totally wrong and missed a segment of the show? Mommy! In retrospect, I realize that instead of threatening them, I should have given my children choices and then let them deal with the consequences if they made the wrong choice. But haven't you ever had one of those days or encountered a situation where you just cannot tolerate any more whining, screaming or fighting? You think you are "going over the edge" and yell so loud that your throat hurts or you see spots. I think the majority of mothers have experienced this at least once in their life. If you haven't, good for you.

I have always considered myself to be a very patient and fair person. However, sometimes my children just did not seem to cooperate or get the point I was trying to get across after many explanations and threats. Then, watch out below, I would blow like Mount St. Helens. It never dawned on me that I was parenting all wrong. In fact, I was deeply offended when my mother-in-law told me that we did not control our first daughter very well. I thought, "How could you say this? Sara is a very good student, uses her manners and is a sweet kid." I wish she would have said instead that our daughter was controlling us. Because a few years later I discovered after reading *Parenting with Love and Logic* by Foster Cline, M.D., and Jim Fay that Sara was controlling us at times and that we would get so frustrated and angry that we would say things we later regretted or even spanked her, which we didn't believe in doing. Obviously, we were not handling situations very well and we were certainly not modeling good behavior for our children.

We have now discovered ways to deal effectively with these issues thanks to advice from pediatricians, other experts in the field and by taking advantage of free parenting classes offered through our school system. I have also solicited information from other mothers who have been successful in tackling these same areas of concern. The following information will hopefully empower you so you do not feel helpless and provide you with techniques that allow you to parent in a loving and reasoning way that will teach your children responsible and appropriate behavior.

Whining

Let's start with whining. You know that sound that starts out slowly, gets a little louder and then a little longer! Well, you can give your child several choices here. You see, it is all about giving your children choices, setting limits, and making them live with their decision. If they make the wrong decision, they get to endure the consequence, not you! Consider these alternatives.

- Tell the children they are welcome to go to their room and whine. They may join you when they are finished whining. Or have a designated chair somewhere for whining only. Give it a name, The Whining Chair! However, tell your child she must remain in the chair the entire time!

- Set a timer for a certain number of minutes given each child's age (i.e., 4-year-olds = 4 minutes; 2-year-olds = 2 minutes). The child can whine until the timer goes off.

- Hold your ears until the child calms down and tell him he is hurting your ears with that sound.

- Tell them you will listen to them when they can talk to you in a voice you can understand. I tell my daughters, "I have no idea what you are talking about when you whine like that. Use your words in a way so mommy can understand you."

- As my friend Dorinda put it one day, "I just ignore it as much as possible." A lot of times she just walks away and tells her children she will listen when they calm down and talk in a normal voice.

- And if all else fails, remember those headphones I suggested you invest in for exercising in Chapter III. Here is where you really put them to use. Tell your children that when you have your headphones on you cannot hear them. Put the headphones on, crank it up and enjoy the sound of music!

Screaming

We were blessed with a healthy energizer bunny in our third child! However, the problem with her was that she learned to scream very loud at an early age! I recall an unforgettable conversation with her pediatrician, Dr. Waters, at her six-month check-up. The minute he walked through the doors, I told him that there must be something wrong with Maria, reporting that she never slept through the night and screamed so much. I point blank said, "You have to help me. She is exhausting me, as well as wearing my nerves very thin." Dr. Waters smiled, gave me a pat on the shoulder and then unloaded the honest truth about the situation, "She will always be an energetic child. I could tell that when she was four months old. And the screaming, well the youngest learns very early on a way to get attention. Her discovery is screaming, so brace yourself, she will probably be a screamer for quite some time." He then added, "I either see a screamer or a very docile child with the third. Just try not to react to the screaming, try your best to ignore it."

Taking it a step further, the headphones were my salvation. Every time she would start that screaming and I was certain she was fine and not in any danger, on went the headphones. Yes, the volume goes loud enough to block out that shrieking sound.

Here again, you can try:

- Saying, "I will talk to you when your voice sounds like mine."

- Whispering, "I will listen to you when you use your inside voice."

- Putting your hands over your ears and say that screaming is hurting your ears.

- Admonishing, "I will listen to you when you calm yourself down."

- And when you cannot take it anymore, ask your husband or somebody else to take over.

Fighting

Bill Cosby once said, "You aren't really a parent until you've had your second child." Parents of one child won't understand this, but parents of two or more children relate to this statement immediately. Cosby was referring to the seemingly constant bickering and fighting that goes on between brothers and sisters. Normal parents who have normal kids have kids who fight. That's one things kids do. Sibling rivalry is part of growing up.

In her article, "Fighting Siblings—What Do I Do?," Shirley King sums it up this way. "Having siblings can provide your child opportunities to learn how to share, how to be a friend, how to love, and get along with others, and how to cooperate among themselves with their brothers and sisters. Thus, there are many positive aspects to family life with more than one child, although many parents might say, "Not in my family!"

King goes on to say that this continual fighting between siblings is a major frustration to parents. They feel that nothing they are doing is working. Parents' typical reactions to fighting include screaming "shut up, you're driving me crazy!," taking sides, issuing threats and accusations, dismissing negative feelings, and solving children's problems for them. All of these reactions only add fuel to the fire! Instead of reacting to the fighting, parents can choose to be proactive as illustrated in the following examples.

- Parents can stay out the fights in a nonjudgmental way. Children need to be able to settle things for themselves. Parents can teach negotiation skills later during a calm period. Teach your child to say, "I'll give you these blocks for those." This will help them learn win-win skills that will be useful now and in the future.

- Parents can show confidence that their children will work things out. "I see two children and one doll, and I know you two can work things out together so both of you are happy." Believe it and walk out of the room. You'll be surprised how often it works.

- In the same situation, the parent can get down on the children's level and lovingly put a hand out. Most of the time, they will give you the toy. Carol DeVeny, an in-home daycare provider, was skeptical at first. However, she reported that the two toddlers stopped the fight, gave her the toy, and said "We share, mommy."

- Many mothers suggest separating the children by telling them they have a choice to make. They can either play together nicely or go to their rooms and play quietly alone.

- And finally, parents need to remember to affirm and accept their children's feelings.

All feelings are O.K., but not all actions are. A parent can say, "You felt very angry at your sister because she broke your truck. You can tell her that with words, not by hitting. Bodies are not made for hitting." Keep in mind that the bad feelings need to come out before we can get to the good feelings.

When parents react to hostility with hostility, they are unwittingly promoting sibling rivalry. Future generations will need the skills of negotiation and cooperation in their businesses and personal relationships. As parents we can begin now to teach our children these important skills. Think what an incredible difference this can make in their lives!

Here is an overall good reminder for dealing with the whining, screaming and fighting! A social worker once told me that you can:

- *Beat it* . . . leave the room or area, find a closet or bathroom to hide in.

- *Bear it* . . . just stand there and ignore it.

- *Boom out* . . . put on your headphones, turn up your radio or stereo and block those irritating sounds!

So feel empowered now to deal with your children during those challenging and frustrating times that are bound to happen. I encourage you to take advantage of parenting classes in your area. Local schools, hospitals, churches and community centers usually offer classes. Parenting can be enjoyable when you learn some basic techniques and positive ways of communicating to your children.

And don't forget to praise your children when they are behaving in a nice way toward one another. Tell them, "I was really proud of the way you shared your toys with Kurt." "I really like the way you are playing with your sisters." Catch them doing something good and tell them!

Use your calm words, not hands, when trying to discipline your child. And if you feel the need to spank, then use the one-spank-only rule. Only spank one time and get the child's attention. Don't beat yourself up because you have used spanking as a means of discipline. Most of us have been there and sometimes done it out of frustration. This chapter gives you ideas and alternatives for dealing effectively with these challenging moments.

After eight years of parenting and feeling frustrated at times, sometimes even questioning my ability as a mother, I have found through reading and using the suggestions of experts and other mothers that I can anticipate situations and deal effectively with them. I now handle them with more reason and in a loving way.

Finally, I'd like to share some of what I've learned. From *Kids Are Worth It* by Barbara Coloroso, remember these thoughts:

- Influence and empower, not control and make mind
- Encouragement, not bribes and rewards
- Discipline, not punishment

What kids need, instead of being told what to think, is lots of information about themselves and the world around them, as well as opportunities to make decision, including some less-than-wise ones. As long as their decisions are not life-threatening, morally threatening, or unhealthy, let your children's choices and the consequences of those choices be their own to grow with and learn from.

Self-trust is one of the first steps toward becoming a responsible, resourceful, resilient, human being. As Faith Baldwin in *Kids Are Worth It* has said, "Character builds slowly, but it can be torn down with incredible swiftness." Children don't need many "Nos," many mini-lectures, unnecessary questions, empty threats, ultimatums, put-downs, warnings or dictates. What they need instead is support, explanations, encouragement, opportunities to be responsible and invitations to think for themselves!

> *The main source of good discipline is growing up in a loving family, being loved and learning to love in return.*
>
> Dr. Benjamin Spock, *Baby and Children*

Chapter VIII

Pick Your Battles!

"**P**ick your battles," my friend Susan told me when we were having trouble taking our oldest, and the only child at the time, with us into stores when shopping. "Pick your battles," our middle daughter's preschool teachers reiterated when I tried apologizing for my daughter wearing the same short jumper with question- able, matching T-shirts for three months in a row.

Why didn't I remember those three important words when my husband suggested going to a local restaurant on the way home from a daylong trip of apple picking? It had been an enjoyable trip and the children had displayed decent behavior all day. However, they did not have naps and emphatically stated that they wanted to go home and eat. But John assured me we would get in and out of the restaurant in a timely manner. "Okay," I reluctantly agreed.

I should have known from the beginning that we were doomed. On arrival, the hostess announced they were out of colors, activity sheets and stickers. "What, no stickers?," the littlest one exclaimed. And, since I was not prepared for this sudden stop, I had not brought any back-up activities for the children. The hostess soon introduced us to Susie, the wait-ress-in-training, "Oh, by the way," she said, "Tonight is my first night of waitressing and I'm so scared." Great, I think to myself, this is not starting off very well at all.

At the time, we were the only ones in the restaurant. However, by the time we got our food, the restaurant was full, the service was poor, and the food appeared to come out one plate at a time! Needless to say, I was stressed to the "max," the kids were restless and started fighting about who was sitting too close to whom, the youngest started chanting "I want to go home, I want to go home," and then—boom—she fell off the booster chair and hit her head on the way down. So we not only had squirming children, but a howling one as well! Do I need to describe how I was feeling at this point? Probably not, but I will. I was so embarrassed and frustrated that I just wanted to crawl out of that restaurant . . . no, I wanted to slither out with a paper bag over my head.

Most of all, I was upset at myself for not going with my original "gut feeling" of, "no way," when my husband suggested eating out! My real feelings and thoughts were, "No, I don't think eating out is a good idea. We have been gone all afternoon. The kids are tired and hungry, and the best solution is to take them home, let them relax and eat in their own environment." Does the above sound familiar to you? Remember, Mother does know best!

Checking Your Child's Tolerance Level

We need to do a quick assessment of our children when situations like this arise. Ask yourself, are they tired? Is it close to nap time or have they missed a nap or stayed up too late the night before? Are they hungry? Is it close to meal time? Should I have given them a cracker or drink to hold them over? Are they stressed? Have they been expected to go on one too many errands with you? Have you been traveling a lot and they're off their schedule? Have they had a busy day filled with preschool activities, and so forth?

If the answer is "yes" to any of the above questions, be understanding and don't push them. Say something like, "I know you are tired of running errands with mommy, but thank you for being so good. Let's go home and fix lunch now."

My friend Tracy put it this way, "Try to use an 'ounce of prevention' by keeping regular mealtimes and bed times, not missing naps, and bringing snacks along. Try not to overdo it! Keep errands to one or two stops and not too many hours of shopping."

Case in point: When I was at the grocery store one Saturday afternoon, I noticed a family of four. Mom, dad, a little boy around two and a half and a baby who was probably six months old. The boy started crying, "I'm tired, mommy, I want to go home." His mother leaned over and said something to him. Then the dad took the little boy behind the candy counter and spanked his little hand so hard it made him wail! I looked at my watch. It was after 1:00 p.m. Yes, he was probably tired and needed to be home taking a nap, not doing the weekly grocery shopping. It took everything I had not to go over and tell the father that he was the one who needed the spanking, not the child.

However, if the assessment shows the opposite—that the children are fed, well rested and not stressed—give them choices and explain to them what you are going to do. "We need to run two errands this morning and after we run some errands we will come home and play in the sandbox."

Here are some words of wisdom from some experienced mothers.

- "Remember, in all phases and stages of raising children, being consistent is very important. That way the child knows that you mean what you say. Sometimes it is easier to let children have their own way, but once you do, you have started to lose control. When you want the child to do something, don't add O.K? at the end of the sentence.

  For example, "It's time to go to bed, O.K.?" When you do that, you are giving the child the option to say, "No." (Kristi Plumb, a successful mother of three college-aged daughters)

- Lori Lang gave this bit of advice. "Speak to your children in a normal, calm voice and tone. Do not use baby talk or yell. They will listen to your reasoning better." (mother of two grade-school-aged children)

- "First of all, remember that some things are just stages. Don't lecture, be short and to the point!" (Susan Ashby, mother of three young children)

- "I have found that giving choices helps. If a child has the opportunity to pick between two choices, the correct behavior or action is usually chosen." (Marcia Poikey, mother of three young children)

- Claudia Beckmann has found a strategy that works for her children. It is the "1, 2, 3" approach. She will set the expectation and tell them she will count to 3 and by the time she gets to 3 they will have done or will be doing what she told them to do!

- Denise Tinkham added these thoughts, "When dealing with certain situations, give your children hugs, kisses and praise when they perform the task appropriately. Use positive reinforcement to bring about the desired outcome. Do not use bribes or threats." (mother of two children)

Here's something to remember before we look at different issues that children like to challenge: Every child is different and what works for one may not work for another. Don't be hard on yourself if your approach doesn't work immediately. Keep trying and realize that some days are better than others. It is like my dear friend, Melody Marshall, reminded me one day . . . "Mama said there would be days like this!" But do not give up after just one or two attempts. Be consistent and persistent!

Clothing Wars

I love this one. Almost every mother interviewed mentioned this issue. So, what do you do?

- It doesn't work to force your children to wear something they don't like. Take them shopping (one at a time) and choose clothing together. When setting out clothing for the day, give them a choice between two outfits. However, remember she may want to wear that favorite short jumper. Let her wear it if it is clean and doesn't show off her panties. If it is too short, but still fits, let her put shorts underneath. There will come a time when the favorite jumper simply will not fit any more and that is the time children find another favorite outfit or even choose the outfit you want them to wear.

- Try this idea for age appropriateness:

    Age Two – Give the child a choice between two outfits, allowing her to feel as if she has chosen what she wished to wear.

    Age Three – The child picks an outfit one day, you select the other day.

    Age Four – Allow the child to choose his outfit, as long as it is weather appropriate. This is a way of allowing him to assert his independence and individuality.

- If the child enjoys one particular outfit, let her wear it as long as it is clean. If it is not appropriate for the weather or a given situation (like church), then give her a choice. Say, "Anna, you can either wear those shorts and T-shirt after Sunday School or tomorrow when we will be at home. Let me know what you decide about that, so we can pick out a dress for Sunday School."

- If you have clothes hanging in the closet that he will not wear, take them back and get a refund if you still have the price tags. Better yet, do not cut price tags off new clothes until you are certain the he is going to wear the clothes. Also, tell grandparents or whoever else may purchase clothing for the child that he is going through a phase and that it is better not to buy clothes for a while. If they do anyway, accept the clothing graciously, saying that he may not wear it but that the younger sibling, if of the same gender, will enjoy wearing it in a few years.

- If children want to wear shorts in the winter and are determined to do it, let them try it one time. They usually learn very quickly that once is enough.

Temper Tantrums

Has your child ever had one? In public? Don't feel you are alone. Many children try it at least once, twice, or maybe more times until they learn it doesn't work! Here are some ways for you to consider as you tackle this high-visibility challenge.

- A social worker once recommended this idea. Ask the child if he would like to go to his room or the basement to act like that. Tell him you do not want to see or hear it! Carefully, pick him up or guide him to the area he has chosen.

- Tell your child that you are not going to listen to that kind of behavior and walk away.

  I usually go up to my room and put my headphones on at this point. My other option is to go to my favorite hiding place in the house—my closet. Sometimes I walk to the garage or go outside, take a deep breath, count to ten and tell myself to hang in. She will quit sooner or later!

- If we are out in public, I give my children a choice. They can either stop acting that way or we will have to leave. They probably will not be able to reason here, so you calmly pick them up or take their hands, saying, "Sara, this is unacceptable behavior, so let's go home." On the car ride home, don't say a word. Wait until later when everyone is calmed down, then discuss the tantrum situation. Say something like, "I would really like to take you shopping with me again. But I will not be able to take you if you choose to behave like that again." Try it again, but be prepared because the child may very well throw another tantrum. Be consistent with your response and say the same thing. Children soon learn that this behavior does not work. It helps if you establish, up front, why you are shopping. For example, "We are not buying anything except bread or milk today." Or, "I need to get some milk and you may pick out a package of gum." The tantrum involves a toy, I say, "That will be a good idea to put on your birthday or Christmas list. Which one should we put it on?"

- One mother says that when the children get to a "point of no return," she warns, "Don't you dare even think about smiling. Now don't smile. I said you could not smile." She alleges that this approach sometimes helps her children escape from their anger.

Potty Training

Potty training does not have to be an unpleasant experience between you and the child. It can be a positive experience if you remember this bit of information:

- Some children are easier to train than others.

- There are those children who are ready at age two and those who developmentally are not ready until much later.

- It is important to keep the feelings around potty training enjoyable and positive.

- When a child is ready, he or she will show signs. "Mom, I want to go on the potty," or "Mommy, I want to wear big girl panties or big boy pants." "I just pottied in my diaper," they may say. This is the time to start. Children must be ready. Don't force it.

- When they go without an accident, praise them. Tell them you are proud of how hard they are trying to go on the big potty or their little potty. Use positive, rein-forcing words. Do not get upset if they have an acci-dent. Refrain from making negative comments which will only frustrate them and hinder progress. Tell them that it is all right and that it happens to everyone. Clean it up and move on.

- Put them in regular training pants, so if they have an accident, they will feel how uncomfortable it is to be in wet underpants.

- What about a setback when a new baby arrives, for example? It can happen. Our oldest daughter was completely trained before the second one arrived. However, one day she announced to me while I was changing the baby that she was going to start wearing diapers again. My comment was "that would be fine." She eventually changed her own mind and decided she didn't want to be a baby anymore.

Food Battles

This section on food battles was taken from *Kids Are Worth It!* by Barbara Coloroso.

- Kids learn to listen to their own bodies at an early age. They know when they are full and try to tell us. We don't always listen. The baby spits the bottle out of his mouth and you push it back in. The two-year-old pushes her plate away and you play airplane to get her to open her mouth (and all she has to do is shut the hangar door and you're stuck).

- Forcing kids to eat when their bodies tell them they are full gives the message, "What your body tells you doesn't count. I know what you need and don't need." But you don't. When kids say they are full, believe them. When they push food away, don't push it back. Much more than nutrition and table manners are at stake.

- At mealtime give choices, but make sure they are practical and ones that you can live with. You could say, "Do you want half a sandwich or whole?" Not, "What do you want to eat for lunch?"

- Give options with limits. If she says she wants a whole sandwich, don't remind her that yesterday she ate only a half. Why did you ask her if you already knew what you wanted her to say? How would you feel if you went to a restaurant, ordered the deluxe salad and were told, "Last week you needed a doggie bag for that. Maybe you ought to order the mini this time!"

- After asking them if they want a whole or half a sandwich, prepare it. If they say they want a whole sandwich and eat only half, say, "No problem. I will wrap it up so you may have it for a snack before your next meal."

- The goal here is to let your child know that he can listen to his own body and that you will respect what it tells him. At the same time, you recognize that he can make a mistake with regard to the amount of food he takes and can deal responsibly with the mistake.

- Do you have a toddler who doesn't like cooked vegetables? Give her frozen corn, frozen carrots, and frozen peas for a snack. You'll probably find that she will eat lots. Frozen corn, carrots and peas do not taste like corn, carrots or peas. They taste frozen.

- Do you have a child who dawdles with his food? Don't nag him. Just say, "We'd love to eat with you. We'll be here for ten more minutes. If you're not finished, we will let you eat in peace and quiet." Let him finish eating by himself and carry his dishes over to the sink and load the dishwasher if he is old enough. Avoid nagging, begging and bribing. If a child eats slowly, it should be his responsibility and not your problem.

- Do you have a child who, if given the opportunity, would eat only macaroni and cheese every meal, every day? You can make up a meal calendar and let her mark five meals during that week. Who said macaroni and cheese wouldn't taste good for breakfast? You can take this opportunity to show your child how to vary the recipe, the method of cooking it, and the ways to serve it, all while celebrating her love of two basic food groups combined. This beats the alternative of refusing to let her have macaroni and cheese and her refusing to eat any other food you put in front of her.

- Picky eaters, for the most part, come from panicky parents. Most kids would not have a problem with food if we didn't worry so much about it. But we worry, worry, worry and they quickly figure out that they have a powerful tool to use to engage us in conflict. (If you have a picky eater, don't serve a casserole to him. He knows that you put something in there that he doesn't like and he's bound and determined to find it.)

- Food conflicts can be reduced by following simple guidelines:
  — Have a variety of good foods in the house and eat those foods yourself.
  — Teach your children about the food they are eating.
  — Let your children help plan and prepare well-balanced meals and nutritious snacks.
  — Eat a variety of meals served in a variety of ways.
  — At least once a month have a formal celebration with your children.
  — Teach your children cultural or religious customs that have been in your families for years.
  — Teach your children manners.

— Teach your children how to shop for groceries and about budgeting.

— Teach your children to cook!

Shopping or Errands

Believe me, this can be a fun time! However, you need to communicate with your children about the shopping trip before you set off on such an adventure.

• Tell them where you are taking them and why you are going. Children need to learn at a young age that they do not get something every time they go shopping. Tell them they can look at things, or, if they have money from gifts or allowances, they may purchase something. When they ask if they can have something, I usually say, "Not today, honey. We can put that on your birthday or Christmas list. Which would you like to do?"

They most always will make a choice. However, be prepared if the approach doesn't work. There may be one toy that they can't imagine living without. They may stand in the aisle and start pouting. Watch out for the tantrum that may come next. Be firm and do not give in! Say, "Nathan, you can either put the toy back on the shelf or we will have to leave." He cannot rationalize at this point. Gently take the toy and place it back on the shelf. Take your child's hand or pick him up and say in a calm voice, "It is time to go home." Do not bribe, threaten or demean him. Just remain calm.

At this point I usually put a nice smile on my face, especially if everyone is staring or glaring at me. You see, they all have just had a memory lapse. They have either forgotten moments in their lives when their children did this or they never took their children anywhere. So continue in your calm demeanor, check out if you have items you really need to purchase, and then leave the store promptly. Do not say anything to your child about the incident. However, if he is still carrying on about the toy, say, "I will listen to you when you calm down."

After one or maybe a few more explosions like this in a store, children usually learn that this behavior does not get them whatever it is they want at the moment and that it does not bother you either.

- Making shopping an adventure. Tell them they are on a treasure hunt for milk, eggs, bread, and so on. Have them step only on brown tiles in the store. If we don't see anymore brown tiles, then they have to pretend swimming, etc.; have them be creative with this game.

- When you are checking out, give the children a choice. Tell them they may stand either next to the shopping cart or next to you. Let them make the decision. You may need to give the choice again if they become wiggly because you are taking a long time checking out or because the person in front of you got an item without the price tag!

Phone Time

Oh boy! Have you ever experienced a phone call where the children decide to make it the most miserable time of your life? I've been there and do not like being there. So what do you do? (Besides lock yourself in a closet.)

- Remind your children not to interrupt while you are talking on the phone. Make this an agenda item and discuss it during your family meetings. (I discuss family meetings more in Chapter X.) Role play this situation with your children, if necessary. Have them pretend to talk on the phone to Grandma. Keep interrupting them so they realize what it feels like. Older children understand this very well. Younger ones catch on quickly with some rehearsing. When they learn not to interrupt, which does take some practicing on their part, praise them. Tell them when you get off the phone, "Jesse, I really appreciate your not interrupting me while I talked to Mr. Smith." Make sure you also praise them in your family meeting.

- For younger children, have a drawer or play box close by to give them when you are on the phone. This should distract their attention for a while, unless you get long-winded. If you are going to be on the phone, tell them ahead of time. Ask them if they need anything. Suggest an activity if they are not doing anything, and remind them not to interrupt you. Remember, you have to practice this a few times before it becomes a habit for the child not to interrupt.

Picking up Toys

Make what can be a tedious task into a game.

- "Let's have a pick-up game. See who can pick up toys faster than anyone else."

- Sing a pick-up song. "It's pick-up time. It's pick-up time. It's time to put the toys away!"

- Give a choice, such as, "You may go outside and play as soon as your toys are put away."

- And remember, do not forget to praise them. Tell them you like the way they always help picking up and putting away their toys.

Allowances

My dear friend, Dianne Countryman, shared this wonderful and creative way of issuing allowances.

- Every two weeks the children get their allowances— $1 for every year of the child's age. The amount is then broken down into these categories:

Savings:	50%	
Spending:	25%	
Charity:	10%	
Taxes:	15%	(This is a fact of life. They might as well find out now that they cannot keep everything they make!)

Once every month look at the tax jar! (Usually $10 or so has accumulated.) Decide what you, as a family, will spend it on. As an example, it may be pizza out, bowling, a movie or another favorite family activity. Dianne noted she learned this financial strategy from best-selling author Neale Godfrey.

Lenore Schiff, school counselor at my daughter's elementary school, offered this bit of advice about issuing allowances. "Allowances should be given unconditionally and the child should have some autonomy with the money. However, they should be responsible for spending the money wisely and not always on 'things they want'." For instance, she has her children purchase gifts for their parents and siblings out of allowances. She also encourages them to save money either by putting it in the bank or placing it in a secure place at home.

The children are given a set amount of money for vacations. They may spend it any way they desire. However, they are informed that once the money is spent, no more will be given. This is a valuable lesson for teaching them to spend money wisely and enhancing their decision-making skills.

Lenore suggests that families should set certain expectations and specifications when it comes to assigning chores. Chores should also be age-appropriate. As they get older children should be expected to help more around the house with more difficult tasks.

Separation Anxiety and Clinging

Some children go through clinging stages at different times. Usually, it is age appropriate. Did you know it can even occur around five years old? Anna's preschool teachers reminded me of this when Anna started crying and wrapping herself around my leg at age five. Each child goes through some form of separation anxiety around this time in their life. It may be clinging, crying, voicing their decision that they are not going to school, or irritability. This is a way of displaying their anxiety about going off to kindergarten soon.

• Therefore, when you drop your child off at a daycare, preschool or babysitter, give her a quick hug and kiss, tell her you love her, and you will see her later. Hand her over to the teacher or sitter. Sometimes you will have to "peel" the child off of you. Do it quickly and leave, even if the child is screaming and crying. Don't give in. However, do call back and check on them later for your peace of mind. Just a word of caution. If the child becomes withdrawn, really fearful of the situation or voices concern that "they are mean to me, she hits me or slaps me," then listen to your child and investigate immediately.

Getting Dressed

Discuss this routine with your children. Tell them how we all need to get up, get dressed, brush our hair and teeth, and so on, every day. Some children adjust very well to routines and never need reminding. However, others need some help. Parents should not remind children all the time to do this and that. Children gradually need to accept responsibility for themselves. You may need to practice many times or role model this behavior with them.

- Have them put their clothes out the night before.

- Give them a choice such as, "You may watch cartoons as soon as you are dressed," or "Breakfast will be served as soon as you are dressed, hair brushed," and so on. If they still don't get moving, say, "You may wear your pajamas today to preschool or you may choose to get dressed. You decide what you want to do, because I need to drop you off by 9:30 so we are not late." (I say this all the time when my preschooler declares she is not going to school. Guess what? I have never had to take her in pajamas. She eventually chooses to get dressed.)

Giving up the Pacifier

This usually takes a few trials and maybe even some errors.

- Poke a hole with a needle in the tip of the pacifier so it will lose some of its sucking power.

- Tell your child that she is a big girl now and that only babies need pacifiers. Let her place it in a box and put it away. Wrap up a new pacifier and give it to a new baby as a way of reinforcing the idea that pacifiers are for "babies."

- Decrease the use of pacifiers. Tell the child he can only have it at naptime or bedtime. Let him put it in a special place (drawer, dresser, desk, etc.). Limit use to bedtimes. Let him pick a day for throwing the pacifier away and then let him throw it away. You may find the child a few hours later digging through the trash, but you need to stick with your original plan.

- Give the child a choice. Would you rather give the pacifier to a new baby or throw it away?

Hitting, Biting and Pulling Hair

Especially among siblings and friends, these behaviors are hard to avoid. But here are some positive ways of dealing with them.

- Say bodies are not made for hitting, biting or pulling hair. Project this in a calm, but firm voice. Get down on the children's level and talk to them face to face. Say, "We do not allow this in our family." Make them apologize to the person they hurt. Separate the children and tell them to play alone for a while if they cannot play nicely together.

- If they hit or pull hair, say, "It looks as though you have too much energy in your feet or hands." Have them go run around the house a few times. Give them a job to do with their hands. For example, let them clean the windows or doors.

These suggestions should prevent some of these unacceptable behaviors. You must be consistent and keep enforcing the rules. Also praise children daily when they are being good. Say, "I am really proud of you today. You did not hit or pull your sister's hair! You played nicely and were so kind!"

Riding in the Car

Of course, in the car, it's seat belts on at all times. Wear your seat belt, too, to model safe behavior to your children. If they refuse to put the seat belt on, don't start the car but wait until they are buckled in. Tell them, in a nice, calm voice, "We will sit here until the belts are buckled." Don't move until they are on!

While driving, if the children get loud, scream, whine or fight, tell them you will have to pull over because you cannot concentrate on your driving with all the noise. Find a safe place, pull over, and shut off the engine. Sit there until they quiet down. After you have done this a few times, the mere mention of pulling over usually produces a quick quietness among them all!

Naptime

Be consistent. Try to put the child down for a nap at the same time every day.

(Of course, babies' schedules are sometimes unpredictable.) Some children give up their naps early on. If they do, tell them that they will have a quiet or rest time in their room.

They can play or look at books, but discuss with them that you need time to yourself to get a few things done.

Moving into the Big Bed (Giving up the Baby Bed)

When ready, let your child go the store with you to select his new bed or discuss with him and show him the "hand-me-down" bed. Let him pick out his own sheets and pillows. Purchase or check out a few new bedtime stories for his first night in the bed. In the beginning, for every night he successfully sleeps in his bed, praise him—tell him how proud you are of him sleeping in his big bed.

Bedtime

Bedtime doesn't have to be a nightmare! This section is taken from *Kids Are Worth It!* by Barbara Coloroso.

Don't lie to your children. Don't tell them they need their sleep. Be honest with them. You need their sleep, and often you need more sleep than they seem to. You have to decide whether you want them to bed early and wake up early or to bed late and up late. As much as you might like it, you probably can't have them to bed early at night and up late in the morning.

As a family you have to look together at what works best in your home. Because of work commitments and your own body clock, you may prefer to have your young children have a late nap, be up with you later in the evenings and all of you sleep in later in the morning.

Provide a basic bedtime routine that is flexible enough to adjust to the needs of individual family members and the family as a whole.

The responsibility for establishing the routine rests first with the parents, but then, as the children grow older, responsibilities and decisions about bedtime and bedtime routine are increasingly turned over to them. By the time they leave home, the children have a healthy regard for the need to sleep, an understanding of their own body clock, and respect for the needs of those around them. In the give-and-take of family life, they have learned common courtesies and are able to balance their own needs and wants with the needs and wants of those they are living with. Turning the music down so as not to wake up a four-year-old brother can translate into keeping the music down in the room when a college dorm mate is trying to study. Brushing teeth, throwing dirty clothes in the laundry, putting on pajamas, crawling into bed to read a while before turning the light out are habits practiced regularly as a child that don't just disappear when a young adult leaves home.

- Tell the children that they may stay up as long as they stay in their rooms and do not bother mom or dad. Permit them to look at books, read, or listen to music. However, get them up at the same time every day. Do not let them "sleep in"! Therefore, if they choose to stay up late, they will have to deal with the consequences of being tired the next day. It will not take long for them to figure out they need to go "nigh-nigh" on time!

- Where to sleep? Much has been written about where children should sleep. The advice ranges from the family bed to their own beds and never any place else. The truth is that there isn't only one best way; there isn't one right way and a bunch of wrong ways. Each family needs to explore options it is comfortable with, ones that best enable all family members to get the sleep they need along with balancing the need for cuddling, the need for privacy, children's emotional needs, and parents' need for a spontaneous and satisfying sex life.

- Try locking your bedroom door so the children cannot wander into your room at night. I remember my parents doing this. We knew we could knock if we were sick or had a bad dream. Then one of them would escort us back to bed to tuck us in. Occasionally, they would find us asleep outside their door the next morning.

Lastly, establish a bedtime routine. Kids count on some kind of consistency and some sort of structure. Basically they need to take care of their personal hygiene (face and hands washed; maybe a bath or shower with your help, if young; teeth brushed; toilet, if necessary— usually advisable), change into bedtime wear, do something calming to relax (singing, storytelling, reading), dim the lights or put a night light on, and fall asleep.

In summary, do not forget these three important words, "pick your battles!" And remember these words of advice from Terri Clamons.

Don't let rules "rule" your family's life. Role modeling and "let's pretend" role playing go a lot farther in working out the "kinks" of growing up for both children and parents. Remember! "Rules Without Reasons" don't teach or nurture. Some day your child will be making his own rules and needs to know how to reason and process the decisions involved in rule making. The best place for a child to learn "self-rule" or self-discipline is at home with you.

When you "lay down the rules," grab some time and patience and talk it through with your child. Even though he may not completely understand the reason yet, he will know there is a reason. Some day you will see a young adult emerge who is self-disciplined and responsible and respects the reasons for rules—yours and his.

Terri Clamons, author of *Wellfamilies Handbook*, mother of three adult children

Chapter IX

I'm Not the Maid or Short-Order Cook Around Here!

I really find pleasure in preparing meals for my family that are well-balanced and pleasing to the eye. For the most part, the children enjoy them, too!

It was a typical Thursday evening at our house. John had just arrived home and was reading the newspaper. (The necessary wind-down time after a long day at the office.)

The children had informed me that they were getting hungry—"real hungry." They had all perched themselves around the table like little birds. I was waiting for the lasagna to finish baking in the oven, when I asked nicely, "Could you girls please set the table?" No response. Hmmm, I thought, surely they must not have heard me. Again, "Girls, could you please set the table?" That glazed look on their face is still there and no response. Okay, third time is the charm. Patiently, again I reiterate, "Girls, please set the table." Still not a movement.

When the food was ready I assembled it on my plate, poured a glass of milk and sat down to eat. My comment to them at this point was, "I wish all of you could join me for this delicious meal. However, since you chose not to set the table it would be very difficult to eat without a plate or utensils." If only I could have snapped a picture at that point to capture the look of total shock on everyone's face. The oldest got up immediately with a comment of, "Mom, I can't believe you would do this!" The middle one started crying and the little one went over and grabbed the napkins. Oh, and the big one, my husband, decided to slide out of his easy chair and help as well.

Not moving an inch and savoring every bite, I watched with astonishment how they quickly set the table, filled their plates and poured a drink. My point was proven. Need I say more? Every time that I remotely mention that the table needs to be set, guess what—they are moving as fast as they can!

Responsibility is the key word here. It finally dawned on me, from the instance above, that my children and husband were not accepting enough responsibility around the house. So, from that day forward I vowed I would not be a servant to my family!

The realization occurred to me that I was obligating myself to the family. My intentions were good; picking up all the time so my house appeared organized and neat, preparing meals, setting the table and cleaning up, proving my family eats good and nutritionally balanced meals, reminding them to do this and that so they wouldn't forget, getting them everything they demanded, and on and on. But quite frankly, I was running myself ragged and getting very frustrated because I felt no one appreciated me! I was being taken for granted—no wonder mothers say their role is viewed as a "thankless job"! Well, hello—I created this mess, so it was time to fix it!

Responsibility

In giving your children too much and expecting too little in return, well-intentioned parents often fail to instill in their children an adequate sense of family loyalty and obligation. In generations past, parents expected a lot of their children. They expected children to keep themselves occupied, do their own homework, make decent grades, demonstrate respect for adults and perform chores in and around the house.

Many of today's parents, by contrast, tend to expect a lot of themselves and relatively little of their children. Unfortunately, some mothers become martyrs to their children. They believe it is their job to keep their children occupied, enroll them in endless activities, help with homework, and see to it they make good grades. They undermine their children's respect for adults by defending them when they get in trouble, blaming teachers for their poor performance in school, and they complain that their children "won't lift a finger around the house," but do nothing about it.

Parents should stop acting so obligated and begin obligating their children.

So how do we obligate our children so they will take responsibility and be prepared for the real world? It is one of the greatest gifts we can give our children. It means teaching them responsibility and decision-making at a young age.

So how do we teach our children responsibility? We should make children accept responsibilities at a very young age. With our first daughter, we did not adhere to this rule very well. We tended to do everything for her. I picked up her toys, picked out her clothes, cleaned her room, reminded her to brush her hair, and on and on I would go, reminding her to do this and that. So when she hit the ripe age of six we had a child who thought her house had a maid service and a short-order cook exclusively for her! And she had two little sisters with big eyes and ears who were taking this all in! Sara's room was a disaster and some days she would try to trot off to school with hair that looked like it had been ratted for hours!

So what did I do? I finally realized that I had been "rescuing" my children and not setting enough limits and delegating responsibility. And when they did not act responsibly, I did not impose a consequence.

Rescuing Parents

The "rescuing parent" is very common among mothers nowadays. When I see women like my "old" self, I cringe! However, I believe there are two parts to the "rescuer."

1. Rescuers do everything for their child, as I mentioned above: Reminding them to eat, get dressed, brush their hair, remember their backpack, lunch, etc. And if the child forgets anything like a lunch, jacket or homework, rescuers blaze a trail to the school to deliver it with a big smile on their face. (Yes, I was guilty of this.)

2. The second part of the "rescuer" parent blames everyone else for their child's problems! They blame teachers, other children and adults for their children's problems! They try to make their child look perfect. Have you ever met a perfect child, or a perfect adult for that matter? I haven't. When catered to and protected like this, children never learn to take ownership of any of their problems, which will present major problems for them later on in life.

Of course, there are some circumstances in which a child may need their parent to intervene for them. This is not to be confused with the "rescuer" parent that I discuss.

I know my children are not perfect and at times do not share properly with others, push another child, or talk back to me. So I deal with it. I use it as a time to teach them by discussing the situation or role-playing to reinforce the appropriate behavior. For instance, "Maria, I know you need to share that baby with your cousin Randi. If you cannot share it and play nicely, then we will put the baby up." I'm putting the responsibility on my child and not blaming the other child or making up excuses for the situation.

Not long ago I listened to a psychologist at a parenting seminar talk about the "rescuer" parent. He said that when you rescue a child all her life, that child comes running back to her parents with problems later on as an adult, maybe even with a failed marriage and children. When you rescue your child, you are taking away their decision-making skills as well as cheating them of taking responsibility for themselves.

So you must delegate responsibility and let your children live with the outcomes. It may be a positive experience or it may a very painful and negative experience. However, they made the decision, not you! They will learn from this decision and, if it was an unfavorable outcome, they will make a better choice next time. We need to learn and grow from our experiences in life.

Now let's talk about age-appropriate responsibility. Many parents unknowingly make the mistake of viewing the young child as helpless, dependent, unskilled—in short, extremely vulnerable and in need of constant protection, catering and reassurances of their devotion in order to feel happy and secure. To view a young child in this way is to see her as the sum of her deficits and to view the parent as all-knowing, all-powerful, and all-giving. Naturally, this may make the parent feel important, but it does a disservice to the child. To change this parenting style requires no less than a complete change in the parent's view of childhood. By learning what a child is capable of at different stages of development, parents can provide opportunities for growth.

By eighteen months, most children can say about fifty words (though they may be understandable only to family member). Developmental psychologists, however, estimate that young children understand about five times as many words as they can say. Therefore, by the time a child is two, she may be saying 100 words, but comprehending 500! Most two-year-olds, in fact, understand almost all simple conversation about daily household activities and routines and can express most of their wants to adults. They are usually speaking in two-and three-word combinations, using language to meet their basic needs and to get what they want. Two-year-olds understand "yes" and "no" as well as "who," "what," and "where" questions, and can answer them appropriately.

So let's take a look at some responsibility we should delegate to our young children.

Two-Year-Olds

- Master undressing more than dressing
- Wash hands with supervision and dry appropriately
- Get undressed and get in the tub with supervision
- Take a few swipes with their washcloth during bath time
- Pick up toys and put away in toy box, etc.
- Feed self with spoon and fork
- Start to potty train; some are trained completely during the daytime: Even those in diapers can get a clean one by themselves and throw the dirty one away
- Know where many foods are in the refrigerator or pantry and can get them out

Three-Year-Olds

- Wash their hands and dry them by themselves
- Toilet trained by day, though they may still wet at night
- Dress self and undress rapidly (may still need help with buttons, snaps, and determining front and back)
- Brush teeth with assistance
- Help set table (napkins and silverware)
- Pick up and put away toys

Four-Year-Olds

- Attempt making bed
- Pick up toys
- Dress self
- Put shoes and coat away
- Help set table and clear some dishes
- Brush teeth and take care of washing hands and face
- Clear toys out of tub after bath
- Take care of bathroom needs

Five-Year-Olds

- Empty backpack and put away
- Make bed
- Take care of bathing and brushing teeth with minimal assistance
- Help with packing for a short trip
- Dress self completely

- Set table, clear dirty dishes
- Help with cooking (pour ingredient in a bowl)
- Get drinks if containers are not too wide or heavy
- Help with pets
- Fold clothes and putting away
- Hang up hats, coats and put shoes away
- Empty out waste basket
- Sweep with small broom
- Love to help outside with planting and weeding
- Assist with grocery shopping

Six-Year-Olds

- Put away personal belongings
- Put clothes in hamper
- Keep room tidy and make bed daily
- Should be able to do the bedtime routine independently
- Dress self
- Water household plants
- Help with the grocery shopping and write down list
- Put away groceries
- Help with small repairs

These are some guidelines to follow when instilling responsibility in your children at certain ages. And don't forget to delegate, delegate, delegate! You are not the only one who can do "it" right. Post lists of chores, errands, appointments and activities each week, then "divide and conquer."

Lenore Schiff, school psychologist at my daughter's elementary school, asks her children if they would like to employ her cleaning service when they decide to slack off on their responsibilities around the house. She says, "I would be glad to pick up and clean your room. However, my services are going to cost you."

Personally, I love this idea. We now have Sue's Cleaning Service in our house. I charge them five cents every time I have to pick up shoes, backpacks, toys, clothes, etc. You set the fee and let them know up front if you do the work . . . they get to pay you for it!

Respect

What is respect? Let me start by discussing disrespect. I was at the cross walk with my daughter and her friend after school one day. A fourth-grade boy in front of me was bullying another boy and using a four-letter word. After hearing it for the second time, I replied, "Excuse me, but I would appreciate you not using that word around me or these children." He looked right at me and said it again with much directness and forcefulness. After I recovered from shock, I got this sick feeling of total disappointment and disgust. I thought, "What is wrong with some children today?" Then my daughter whispered in my ear, "He is so mean."

Thinking about this incident off and on all afternoon, I realized that some children nowadays are just plain disrespectful! It is sad, but true! You wonder where children learn this behavior. Sad to say, it goes back to us as parents and how we "role model" in dealing with situations and behaviors. Makes you speculate about where that young boy learned that behavior, doesn't it?

Now don't get me wrong. Most of us have slipped at one time or another and said a few undesirable words when we have stubbed our toe or dropped an entire glass of apple juice on our freshly cleaned kitchen floor. However, people who use four-letter words or the Lord's name in vain on a daily basis need to evaluate whose ears are within listening distance. A professor in college once said, "When people like to swear, it shows their ignorance." And when you swear at another person, you are showing total disrespect for that individual.

Have you ever asked a child what respect means. You will probably get answers like "being polite," "being courteous," "helping other people." Linda and Richard Eyre's adolescent daughter put it this way in their book *Teaching Your Children Values,* "I think it's nice that Prince William calls people 'sir' and I think manners are important, but respect isn't just using the right words and being well-trained. Respect means really caring about how people feel!" Absolutely, she said it so well!

I will probably never forget how I felt when that young boy was so disrespectful to me, as well as to my child and her friend. At the same time, I know how I feel when someone is respectful to me. I feel good about my encounter with that person. I think to myself, he is a good person and has been trained well. His parents must model good, respective behavior to their child and others!

My grandmother and mother always told me, "If you can't say something nice about someone, then don't say it at all." I think this comment goes hand in hand with respect for others.

I like what the Eyres say about respect in their book, *Teaching Your Children Values.*

> *The importance of and basic necessity for respect are self-evident. Respect is the basis and foundation (and often the motivation) for several of the other basic values of life. Children who learn both to implement and to understand the principle of respect will be better members of society, better friends, and better leaders.*
>
> *The teaching of respect is an interesting and somewhat difficult proposition. The main thing to remember is that respect isn't* **given** *consistently unless it is* **received**. *We need first to respect our children (in terms of how we speak to them and how we treat them) and then to absolutely demand that they show respect for us in return. The respect they* **receive** *in the home will be the basis for their own self-respect; and the respect they learn to* **show** *in the home (to family members) will be the foundation on which to build respect for others outside the home.*

General Guidelines

The Eyres elaborate on the meaning of respect by giving the following guidelines.

Extend respect and then expect respect. Create the proper climate for respect in your own home. We often speak to and deal with our children with less respect than we show to strangers. We treat them as though they have no rights and deserve no explanations. We say "because I said so" and we give them no benefit of the doubt and assume they are guilty until proven innocent.

We need to change this, even if it requires imagining that they are strangers and speaking to them accordingly. Use the words "please" and "thank you" more. **Ask** them whenever possible instead of telling them. Ask for their advice or input on things. Respect their opinions.

Once we make this effort, we are in a position to expect (even demand) respect in return. Make it clear that respect includes tone of voice as well as manners. This expectation must be consistent and repetitive. Simply do not allow disrespect in your home.

Give plenty of praise and recognition. Reinforce respectful behavior and encourage its repetition. Make up your mind to watch for opportunities to praise courtesy and politeness during the month. Catch your child doing something right and make a big deal of it. Praise them in front of other family members—and then try to remember to praise them privately, one on one, later the same day.

Give them a chance to correct themselves by saying "Let's start over." This is a good method to correct disrespectful behavior in a positive way. Establish the pattern (and the habit, in connection with consistently not allowing disrespect in the home) of saying, "Let's start over." When a disrespectful answer is given, when someone fails to say "please" or "thank you," say "Let's start over." Then repeat the situation, letting the child do it correctly. Do this with children of all ages. And when necessary, say "Let's start over" to yourself and then repeat your own statement or behavior in a more respectful way.

Teach by your own examples. Show respectful behavior. As always, example is the best teacher. Let your children see and hear you being concerned for the property and rights of others, assisting the elderly, caring for nature, being polite in all situations and showing self-respect in terms of how you look and how you speak of yourself.

In conclusion, I think it is our job to teach our children responsibility and respect for themselves and others. Children learn by watching their role models, which are us—their parents. So I would like to end this chapter with a quote from a dear friend who said to me one day. . .

For eighteen years you are teaching your children to be independent, responsible and respectful individuals.

Cathy Darnell, (One of the nicest moms I know!)

Chapter X

Enjoy Your Children!

Dedicated to my father

I will never forget the words of wisdom my father said to me a week before he died. "Sue, enjoy your life and really enjoy your children. Life on earth goes by so quickly." Until he made that comment to me, I do not think I was *really* enjoying anything!

I think of him often when the children do "those funny little things" or make some profound statement. We all recall moments with our children that we will remember forever!

One morning I was taking my shower—a ten-minute quiet time that I cherish and have told the children not to interrupt unless it is an emergency or something very important. This particular morning I was interrupted by my middle daughter, Anna, flinging open the shower door wanting to show me her prized possession—the longest, slimiest night crawler I had ever seen! She was grinning from ear to ear as she said, "Mommy, look—meet my new friend, Sylvia!"

I hurriedly finished my shower so I could share the excitement with her and quickly found a container so I would not have to hold it. At this point, I quietly laughed to myself and thought of the things in life that children enjoy. And it brought back wonderful memories from my childhood regarding the simple things in life that my grandmother, "Mammy," taught me to appreciate!

We have all heard the saying "Looking at life through the eyes of a child." To recapture this feeling, I have compiled a list of fun things that you and your children might find exciting to do together.

Simple Things

- Watch the sun set together
- Take a nature walk, pick up sticks, leaves, rocks (don't forget to take a bag for the treasures)
- Make mud pies
- Catch a butterfly and set it free
- Teach them to skip a rock across water
- Look for a four-leaf clover (did you ever find one of these as a child?)
- Look at a full moon
- Find the brightest star in the sky
- Look for night crawlers (you might find Sylvia)
- Finger paint a picture with them

- Teach them "Itsy-Bitsy Spider"
- Catch lightning bugs
- Find the big dipper
- Talk about the different types of birds and then point them out while outside together
- Teach them to whistle—don't forget the two-finger method between the teeth, I'm thankful to my brother Randy for teaching me this!!!!!
- Watch a falling star
- Observe a mother cat with her kittens
- Look for frogs (describe how a tadpole turns into a frog)
- Watch a bird build a nest and then watch the eggs hatch
- Play "Go Fish" card game
- Have a tea party
- Play checkers, try Chinese checkers or chess
- Go on a picnic
- Look for lady bugs
- Go fishing
- Collect rocks
- Teach them to play hopscotch!
- Play kick ball
- Look at clouds and ask them what the shapes looks like
- Take a Sunday car ride

- Tell them a story about when you were a little person

- Go apple picking

- Treat them to an ice cream cone . . . get a double dipper!

- Find a duck pond and feed the ducks

- Pop some popcorn and watch your child's favorite movie with him or her. Turn off the lights and pretend you are at the movie theater

- Visit a strawberry patch

- Throw snowballs with your children

- Build a snowman

- Visit a farm

- Go to a petting zoo

- Build sandcastles

- Play marbles

- Fly a kite

- Climb a tree

- Go to a playground and swing together

- Pick flowers and give them to someone special or an older person who lives alone

- Take a walk on the beach and pick up shells

- Put a dandelion under your child's chin and tell them they love butter!

- Give them a butterfly kiss and hear them giggle!

Learning Experiences

There are other things that we as parents can do to help our children learn. I clipped a resourceful article written by Linda Lewis Griffith (Scripps Howard News Service—Published in the *Kansas City Star*). It was titled, "Parents, It's Easy to Help Your Children Learn." It began like this:

"Want to raise smart children? Start with these steps: Be curious about life. Watch a spider build a web outside your toddler's window. Read a book about volcanoes to your kindergartner. Visit a dairy with your 7-year-old. Or study roadbuilding equipment working along the interstate. You'll be broadening your children's base of knowledge while nurturing the attitude that "life is interesting and worth learning more about."

Take your children on family outings. The museum, a children's concert, an art exhibit and a ghost town are only a few of the mentally stimulating activities you can use to enrich your children's minds. Whether you travel across town or across the country, family outings have the added advantage of building your family's bonds as well as your kids' brains.

Include your children in thought-provoking discussions. Talk with your children about current events, religion or school policies. It's a great way to learn their opinions, and a good method to develop their critical and analytical thinking. Avoid the temptation to prove your point or win every debate with your children. The goal is to help your kids formulate and express ideas, not necessarily change their views.

Read to your children. It's never too early to start reading to your tots. Even babies enjoy listening to stories and looking at pictures. They'll learn to view reading as a positive, relaxing activity. And they'll love the time you spend holding them in your arms.

Minimize their exposure to television and video games. There's a strong—and now proven—negative correlation between children's success in school and the amount of TV they watch; a high score in one area almost always means a low score in the other. Encourage alternative fun activities, such as playing games, riding bikes, working puzzles or reading books.

Help your children develop interesting hobbies. Raising tropical fish, building models, collecting stamps, and playing the flute are examples of stimulating, mind-enhancing activities. Your children will have fun as they develop powers of concentration, determination and patience.

Provide a structured environment for your children. Your home needn't be run like a boot camp. But clear guidelines for behavior, regular meal times, ongoing chore assignments and predetermined study times and bedtimes teach kids how to manage their schedules and give them a sense of consistency in their lives.

Be active in your children's school work. Attend parent-teacher conferences. Support your school's PTA. Ask your kids what they are studying. Be available to help with homework. You'll be sending them a powerful message: "I care about your education."

Support your children's strengths. Not everyone is meant to be a brain surgeon. Help your children develop their natural talents and interest, and value their successes out of the classroom as well as in.

Value knowledge, education and success in your household. Make learning and individual achievement top priorities in your home. Praise your kids for being diligent in their intellectual development and setting them on the road to personal success.

Family Time

As a family, devote a certain amount of time each week to what I call "family time."

- It may not occur every night, but make a conscious effort to sit down to dinner as often as possible. This is a great time for communicating with children. In our family each child gets a chance to tell us about the highlight of their day. However, don't ask the question, "Well, how was your day?" Because you will probably hear, "Oh, fine." Instead, ask the question so they will have to expand on their answer. Such as, "Tell me something fun that happened to you today!" Even a two-year-old loves this!

- Around the World, Around the Table is another fun game to play at dinnertime. The exact form this activity will take depends on the ages and interests of your children. Too many kids grow up far too ignorant of geography, both world geography and American. And what better time than dinner, when the family is together, for you to impart a little geographical knowledge to them or for them to impart it to each other.

- If your kids are young, it may be enough to pepper the dinner conversation with tidbits of knowledge: What is the capital of the state we live in? What is the capital of the state Grandma and Grandpa live in?

- If the kids are a little older, you get into more extensive material and ask them to provide it. Perhaps once a week, so it doesn't become a burden, each child can be asked to prepare three minutes worth of information on any location on the map. The information can be gathered from the encyclopedia, a library book, or any suitable source. If you have a globe or atlas, you can bring it to the table for "show and tell."

Whatever form your geographical wanderings take at the dinner table, your kids are bound to get up from the table with the brains as well as their stomachs enriched.

- Many family projects are complex, expensive, require a good deal of materials and a lot of planning and arranging. And then there are other projects that are so simple and cheap (or free) and yet enjoyable and healthful.

As is so often the case, it is sometimes the simplest projects that are among the most-enjoyed and among the most-treasured memories in years to come. What could be more simple than taking a walk? And doctors say it's among the most healthful exercise!

- Our family has what we call a "family meeting" when we feel the need to discuss the weekly agenda, praise behaviors or discuss inappropriate behaviors. I usually make a list throughout the week for the agenda so I will not forget to mention something important. My husband makes it a lot of fun by taking roll and asking for everyone's input. We have even named the meeting!

- I once heard that there are only a few things that children remember about their childhood. One of them is the family vacations. When I think of my childhood, I have happy vivid memories of our vacations. Vacations do not have to be elaborate, expensive trips. We took advantage of the state parks and beaches and went camping. Even a weekend away to a city that has a zoo or children's museum will be an enriching and memorable experience for your family.

Conclusion

Happy, productive, well-balanced children and young adults don't just happen. They are products of their childhood environment, but even more important, they are a reflection of the ways in which they were nurtured. Central to nurturing, as Bob Keeshan (Captain Kangaroo) points out in his book, *Family Fun*, is the quality time parents spend with their children, involving them, challenging their curiosity, and teaching them what lovable and important people they are. Playing with children is an integral part of quality. Playing together not to see who wins, but to learn and grow is an excellent way for families to make great use of precious time and produce wonderful memories!

I would like to end with a poem my friend Susan wrote about memories. It's a poem that I like to pull out and read often.

A Mother's Love

by Susan Ashby

First we were two and now we are three,
Blessedly, we have become a family,
A Mother's love for her child is like one I have never
known,
You are a gift from above that only God can loan,
Time goes more quickly now, as I watch you grow,
I hope you know how much I love you so,
I wonder each night as I tuck you in and say
your prayer,
Did I hug and kiss you enough so you know how much I
care?
Did I take the time to look in your eyes and listen when you
needed me to?
Did we laugh and play enough to satisfy you?
I wonder as you doze what memories fill your head,
I think about the things I should or shouldn't
have said,
I thank God for the night time, for sleep
and dreams,
The promise of morning and new beginnings
it seems,
For you, each new day brings excitement
and wonder,
A new day to learn and discover,
For me, a new day gives me just a little more time,
To build memories together that will last a lifetime.

So, remember, you can do it! Keep focused on the holistic approach to nourish your mental, physical, emotional, social, and spiritual needs. Take the time to enhance your relationships. Utilize the advice and ideas from this book for dealing with your children during these formative and challenging years. Most of all, enjoy your life and your children!

May you find happiness. That is my wish for all mothers!

BIBLIOGRAPHY

Airola, Paavo, M.D., Ph.D. *Every Woman's Book*. Phoenix: Health Plus Publishers, 1979.

Ammer, Christine. *The New A to Z of Women's Health*. Alameda: Hunter House, 1989.

Bee, Helen L. *The Journey of Adulthood*. New York: MacMillan, 1987.

Bliss, Shepherd, ed. *The New Holistic Health Handbook*. New York: Penguin Books, 1985.

Carson, V. *Spiritual Dimensions of Nursing Practice*. Philadelphia, PA: W.B. Saunders Co., 1989.

Carter, Steven, and Sokol, Julia. *Lives Without Balance*. New York: Villard Books, Random House, 1992.

Chapman, L. "Developing a Useful Perspective on Spiritual Health: Love, Joy, Peace and Fulfillment." *American Journal of Health Promotion*, 1987: 12-17.

Cline, Foster, M.D., and Fay, Jim. *Parenting with Love and Logic*. Colorado Springs: Pinion Press, 1990.

Clinton, Hillary. "Boundless Love and Support is the Key to Healthy, Happy Children." *Kansas City Star*, 12 April 1997.

Coloroso, Barbara. *Kids Are Worth It*! New York: William Morrow, 1994.

DeAngelis, Barbara. *Real Moments*. New York: Delacorte Press, Bantam, 1994.

DiBrigida, Lisa M. and Olson, Ardis, M.D. "Depressive Symptons and Work Role Satisfaction in Mothers of Toddlers." *Pediatrics*, September 1994. Vol. 94 No. 3: 363-367.

Ellis, Elizabeth, Ph.D. *Raising a Responsible Child.* Secaucus, N.J.: A Birch Lane Press, Carol Publishing Group, 1995.

Epstein, Peggy. "50 Ways to Say You're Special." *Christian Parenting Magazine*, 31 Oct. 1996: 36-37.

Everett, Melissa. *Making a Living While Making a Difference.* New York: Bantam, 1995.

Eyre, Linda and Richard. *Teaching Your Children Values.* New York: Simon and Schuster, 1993.

Fischer, Joel, and Gochros, Harvey L. *Planned Behavior Changes: Behavior Modification in Social Work.* New York: Free Press, MacMillan, 1975.

"Healthy Weight Maintenance," sponsored by Harvest Crisps and New Garden Crisps Crackers.

Hock, Ellen. "Depression in Mothers of Infants: The Role of Maternal Employment." *Developmental Psychology*, 1990, Vol. 26, No. 2: 285-291.

Keeshan, Bob "Captain Kangaroo." *Family Fun Activity Book.* Minneapolis: Deaconess Press, 1994.

King, Shirley. "Fighting Siblings—What Do I Do?" *Boise Family Magazine*, 1996.

Levinson, Wendy. "Work May Be Good Medicine." *The Lancet*, 21 January 1995. Vol. 345, No. 894: 140-142.

MacGregor, Cynthia. *Creative Family Projects, Games and Activities*. New York: Citadel Press, 1995.

Maslow, Abraham. *Toward a Psychology of Being*. 2nd ed. New York: Van Reinhold Nostrand, 1968.

Moss, G. *Immunity and Social Interaction*, New York: John Wiley and Sons, 1973.

Parent Source. Winter Ed. Newton Upper Falls: TMSI, 1996.

Pender, Nola J. *Health Promotion in Nursing Practice*. Stamford: Appleton and Lange, 1996.

Rosemond, John. "Parents Need to Expect a Lot More of Their Children." *Richmond Times*, 12 May 1996.

Scarr, Sandra. *Mother Care/Other Care*. New York: Basic Books, 1984.

Sentara Childcare Manual. Norfolk: Sentara Home Care Services, 1992.

Spock, Benjamin, M.D. *Dr. Spock on Parenting*. New York: Simon and Schuster, 1988.

Swenson, Richard A., M.D. *Margin, Restoring Emotional, Physical, Financial and Time Reserves to Overloaded Lives*. Colorado Springs: Navpress, 1992.

Warshaw, Robin. "Make Money at Home." *Woman's Day*, 1 February 1997

Witmer, J. Melvin. *Pathways to Personal Growth*. Muncie: Accelerated Development, Inc., 1985.

Worthington, Everett L. Jr. *Marriage Counseling*. Downers Grove: InterVarsity Press, 1989.

About the Author

Susan Dawes is a writer, volunteer, mother and wife. She received her Bachelor of Social Work from Iowa State University and Master's of Education in Psychology from University of Central Oklahoma. She has worked as a care coordination supervisor for home health services and as a social worker for a nursing center. Currently, Susan works from her home.

Over the years she has asked friends, colleagues and professionals to share their experiences and opinions for improving relationships with husbands, children and friends. Her hope is that readers find these suggestions helpful.

When Mom's Happy, Everyone's Happy! is written from a social worker's perspective, although written by a mom. It is a creative guide filled with much honesty, encouragement and some humorous antidotes!

Susan lives with her husband, John, and three daughters in Overland Park, Kansas.

Mail Orders

When Mom's Happy, Everyone's Happy!
by Susan Dawes

Orders must be accompanied by personal check or money order made out to Cardinal House Publishing, Mail order form and check to:

Cardinal House Publishing
P.O. Box 25096
Overland Park, KS 66225-5096
e-mail: cardinalhp@aol.com

Questions? Call (913) 851-2806 or toll free 1-877-437-6667 (MOMS)

(Quantity orders are invited. Call to inquire regarding bulk discount prices.)

Order Form

WHEN MOM'S HAPPY, EVERYONE'S HAPPY!

Name: _____

Mailing Address: _____

City, State, Zip: _____

Phone Number: (   ) _____

Price Per Copy	$14.95
Quantity Ordered	_____
Subtotal	_____
*Sales Tax	_____
**Shipping & Handling	_____
Total	_____

*Please add Kansas sales tax of 6.875% for orders shipped to a Kansas address.
**Please add $3.00 per book for shipping and handling. Allow 30 days for delivery.

Cardinal House Publishing
P.O. Box 25096
Overland Park, KS 66225-5096
Call (913) 851-2806